Dark Matter

Dark Matter

INDEPENDENT FILMMAKING IN THE 21st CENTURY

MICHAEL WINTERBOTTOM

THE BRITISH FILM INSTITUTE
Bloomsbury Publishing Plc
50 Bedford Square, London, WC1B 3DP, UK
1385 Broadway, New York, NY 10018, USA
29 Earlsfort Terrace, Dublin 2, Ireland

BLOOMSBURY is a trademark of Bloomsbury Publishing Plc

First published in Great Britain 2021 by Bloomsbury
on behalf of the
British Film Institute
21 Stephen Street, London W1T 1LN
www.bfi.org.uk

The BFI is the lead organisation for film in the UK and the distributor of Lottery funds for film.
Our mission is to ensure that film is central to our cultural life, in particular by supporting and
nurturing the next generation of filmmakers and audiences. We serve a public role which covers
the cultural, creative and economic aspects of film in the UK.

A catalogue record for this book is available from the British Library.

Library of Congress Cataloging-in-Publication Data

LC record available at https://lccn.loc.gov/2021007712
LC ebook record available at https://lccn.loc.gov/2021007713

ISBN: PB: 978-1-8390-2339-2
ePDF: 978-1-8390-2341-5
eBook: 978-1-8390-2340-8

Designed, edited and typeset by Tom Cabot/ketchup
Printed and bound in India

To find out more about our authors and books visit www.bloomsbury.com and sign up for our newsletters.

CONTENTS

INTRODUCTION

The directors I talk to in this book are not intended to be a representative cross section of directors working in Britain. They are simply people whose films I like and respect. I was lucky that so many people were willing to give up their time to talk to me. This was perhaps because these interviews took place during the Covid-19 lockdown of 2020. Everyone had time on their hands. The interviews took place by Skype or Zoom.

These conversations are not about the films themselves, but about the process of trying to get films made. Each director's experience is unique. But together they maybe give a series of snapshots of both what is possible, and what is not, in the current landscape of British cinema.

My motive was selfish. I had been making films for 25 years and wanted to step back and think about the way I was working. It felt like the best way of doing this was to talk to other directors about their experiences – and this book was a useful excuse. I hope this book is useful for anyone who wants to make films in this country. But above all, having heard the experience of many directors I admire, I hope that the people who administer the public money invested in British cinema might listen to, and think about, what these directors have to say.

As I started to think about the people I wanted to talk to, I began to think about how few films, or, how few British films, they had made.

- Paweł Pawlikowski's first film was *The Stringer* in 1998. He has made two films in Britain since then, the last being *My Summer of Love* in 2004.

- Steve McQueen's first film, *Hunger*, was in 2008. That is the only British film he has made.

- Lynne Ramsay's first feature was *Ratcatcher* in 1999. Since then she has only made one other British independent film – and that was *Morvern Callar*, 18 years ago.

- Joanna Hogg has made four films (and is currently in post-production on her fifth).

- Asif Kapadia's first film was *The Warrior* in 2001. Since then he has only made two fiction films based in the UK.

- James Marsh has made four British (fiction) films.

- Andrew Haigh's first fiction film was *Weekend* in 2011. He has made one film in Britain since then.

- Carol Morley has made two fiction films in Britain.

- Edgar Wright directed *Shaun of the Dead* in 2004. Since then he has made two more films in Britain (though he is currently editing another: *Last Night in Soho*).

- Stephen Daldry has made three films based in the UK.

- Ben Wheatley has made seven films.

- Peter Strickland has made four films.

There are exceptions of course.

- Danny Boyle has made 11 films based in the UK.

- Mike Leigh's first film was *Bleak Moments* in 1971. Since then he has made 12 more films here in the UK.

- Ken Loach's first film was *Poor Cow* in 1967. Since then he has made another 21.

It may, or may not, be coincidence that the two most prolific directors began their careers 30 years before the end of the twentieth century.

I am not suggesting that the low numbers of British independent films made by each director necessarily represent a series of tragedies for the individual involved – or even a long, drawn-out, melancholy struggle. Many directors have simply moved on to studio movies, or gone to America, or switched to television or theatre. As the conversations in this book show, many are perfectly happy to have made the number of films they have made.

But surely it is a problem for British independent cinema itself, that even successful directors, like the ones in this book – have made so few British films.*

For centuries astronomers have tried to understand our universe by observing the stars shining in the night sky. But now we know – or think we know – that 85% of all the material in the universe is dark matter. This dark matter is impossible for us to see, but without it we believe many galaxies would fly apart. It shapes our universe.

---

* There were some directors who, for various reasons, I wasn't able to interview: Andrea Arnold, Clio Barnard, Shane Meadows, Martin McDonagh and Jonathan Glazer. But if they had taken part, it wouldn't have increased the average number of films made. Martin McDonagh has made one film based in the UK, Jonathan Glazer two, Andrea Arnold three, Clio Barnard three (though she is finishing a fourth) and Shane Meadows, having been fairly prolific in the first few years of this century, hasn't made a film for cinema since 2009.

It occurred to me there might be an interesting parallel in cinema. I know from my own experience that the films a director makes are only a percentage of the films that she or he has tried or wanted to make. At first this seemed like it might be an interesting way of looking at the work of individual directors. But the more I thought about individual directors, the more it seemed like the dark matter of unmade films might help to explain the wider landscape of British independent cinema in the 21st Century.

BRITISH INDEPENDENT CINEMA

It is probably worth saying that I understand that this is a pretty slippery description. You only have to look at BAFTA nominations over the years to realise that 'British' can be applied in pretty strange ways. 'Independent' is an odd term to apply to films that are often in whole, or in part, funded indirectly by the government through institutions like the BFI, Film4 or the BBC… or by people trying to reduce their tax bill. And cinema itself overlaps with television. That is especially true now in the age of platforms like Netflix – but in my experience it has always been the case. The first time I went to Los Angeles was to meet with agents. I had just shown a film at the Toronto Film Festival called *Family*, written by Roddy Doyle. It had been made as a four-hour TV series for the BBC – and we had then cut a two-hour version for the film festival. It had gone down well and distributors wanted to buy it for a theatrical release in the US. I remember being told, slightly hysterically, by an agent not to describe it as television – but as a movie. TV in those days was still a slightly dirty word in Los Angeles.

In the end, Roddy preferred the four-hour version and so we didn't sell the film in the US and *Family* is, therefore, a TV series in perpetuity – not a film.

Michael Winterbottom on set, *Greed* (2019). (photo: Phil Fisk)

THE STARTING POINT

The first time I directed anything 'professionally' was when I was 26. I was given the chance, by a man called Alan Horrox at Thames TV, to try and make something about Ingmar Bergman. Bergman was about to be 70 years old, and his publisher was releasing his autobiography – *The Magic Lantern.*

When Alan offered me this chance I thought I was pretty familiar with Bergman's work – after all, I'd seen maybe ten of his films in the cinema, or on TV. It turned out that this was a small fraction of his work.

Bergman had made more than 50 films, as well as running Dramaten, the Swedish equivalent of the National Theatre, and directed more than a hundred plays.

I spent the next six months going backwards and forwards to Sweden, watching his films and his home movies in the Swedish Film Institute, and meeting and interviewing the people who had worked with Bergman. He had a small team of regular collaborators, actors and crew who worked with him time and time again. Of course, this team evolved over the decades, but it evolved organically from one film to the next.

Bergman would write a script in the autumn whilst working in the theatre, already knowing his cinematographer, his editor, his producer, his line producer, his actors, his budget, his location and so on. In the summer, during his holiday from the theatre, he would shoot his film. More than 50 movies, one a year – he even, occasionally, shot two in the same summer.

That represents, for me, the Ideal. The dream of how filmmaking should be.

The experience also showed me getting films made is often down to luck.

I was lucky Alan offered me the chance in the first place. Then I was fortunate that someone told me that Bergman is a stickler for punctuality.

So when I called him I made sure it was exactly – almost to the second – the time we had arranged.

Then, when I met him in his office at Dramaten, Bergman told me that he had agreed to meet me because of my name. Apparently there was a German farce shown on Swedish TV every Christmas and one of the main characters was called Mr Winterbottom. So that is how I got to make two films about Ingmar Bergman.

Ingmar Bergman wasn't the first director I had had the chance to meet.

A year or two earlier Kevin Brownlow and David Gill had produced a short series of films on British cinema, directed by Alan Parker, Sir Richard Attenborough and Lindsay Anderson. Kevin and David gave me the chance to work as a junior researcher with Lindsay.

As a teenager I had watched Lindsay's films on TV. I was a big fan of *If....* and *O Lucky Man!* So it was fantastic to get a chance to work with, or rather for, Lindsay.

Characteristically, Lindsay's documentary on British cinema actually focussed on his own films, and those of the Free Cinema movement, which he had helped start in the late Fifties.

Lindsay was roughly the same age as Bergman – a little younger perhaps, but Lindsay had only directed a handful of films. That doesn't take anything away from *This Sporting Life*, or *If....* or *O Lucky Man!*, but it seemed to me at the time that it was strange that Lindsay hadn't made more films.

Working with Lindsay was a lot of fun. I remember he would come into the office singing Wham! songs – he was making a documentary about their tour of China. But somehow he had managed to get into a big argument about the film, so there were a lot of complicated games going on between Lindsay and either the band or the people paying for the film. Lindsay seemed to enjoy the complications, the arguments. So maybe that, in some part, explains why he made so few films. Maybe. Of course, Lindsay had a career in theatre as well as cinema. But so did Bergman.

Would British cinema in the Sixties and Seventies be richer if Lindsay had made fifteen films rather than five?

Yes.

MORE IS MORE

Bergman is in many ways an exceptional filmmaker.

But in terms of the number of films that he made, he isn't quite as exceptional as he might seem looking back from 2020. Today it is easy to assume that a 'serious' or 'creative' filmmaker takes three or four or five years to make a film. That a career 'naturally' adds up to a handful of movies. But if you look at a different time and a different place you can see a very different story.

When I started watching films as a teenager I loved the great European directors of the Fifties, Sixties, and Seventies. Many were incredibly prolific. Jean-Luc Godard made 18 films in one decade in France; Truffaut, 21 films in total; Fellini, 24 films; Fassbinder made 21 films before he died at the age of 37.

And often the most prolific periods coincide with their greatest films.

In one decade Bergman made:
Summer with Monika (1953), *Sawdust and Tinsel* (1953), *A Lesson in Love* (1954), *Dreams* (1955), *Smiles of a Summer Night* (1955), *The Seventh Seal* (1957), *Wild Strawberries* (1957), *Brink of Life* (1958), *The Magician* (1958), *The Virgin Spring* (1960), *The Devil's Eye* (1960), *Through a Glass Darkly* (1961), *The Pleasure Garden* (1961), *Winter Light* (1963), *The Silence* (1963)… in addition to all his theatre work.

In six years at the beginning of the Sixties Godard made:
À bout de souffle (1960), *Une femme est une femme* (1961), *Vivre sa vie* (1962),

Le Petit soldat (1963), *Le Mépris* (1963), *Bande à part* (1964), *Une femme mariée* (1964), *Alphaville* (1965), *Pierrot le Fou* (1965), *Masculin Féminin* (1966), *Made in U.S.A.* (1966). As well as a handful of shorts.

In less than a decade Truffaut made:
Les quatre cents coups (1959), *Tirez sur le pianiste* (1960), *Une histoire d'eau* (with Godard) (1961), *Jules et Jim* (1962), *Antoine et Colette* (1962), *La Peau douce* (1964), *Fahrenheit 451* (1966), *La Mariée était en noir* (1968), *Baisers volés* (1968).

Within 10 years in the Fifties and Sixties Fellini made:
I vitelloni (1953), *La strada* (1954), *Il bidone* (1955), *Nights of Cabiria* (1957), *La dolce vita* (1960), *8½* (1963). As well as a handful of shorts.

In the space of four years at the beginning of the Seventies Fassbinder made:
Beware of a Holy Whore (1971), *The Merchant of Four Seasons* (1972), *The Bitter Tears of Petra von Kant* (1972), *Eight Hours Don't Make a Day* (1972), *The Tenderness of Wolves* (1973), *Ali: Fear Eats the Soul* (1974), *Effi Briest* (1974), *Fox and His Friends* (1975). As well as several TV films.

At the same time – and in pretty much the same place – Wenders made:
The Goalkeeper's Fear of the Penalty (1972), *The Scarlet Letter* (1973), *Alice in the Cities* (1974), *The Wrong Move* (1975), *Kings of the Road* (1976), *The American Friend* (1977).

And in the same decade Herzog made:
Even Dwarfs Started Small (1970), *Aguirre, the Wrath of God* (1972), *The Enigma of Kaspar Hauser* (1974), *Heart of Glass* (1976), *Stroszek* (1977), *Nosferatu the Vampyre* (1979), *Woyzeck* (1979).

These clusters of films and filmmakers at certain times and places suggests that it is not just that one filmmaker has suddenly got a lot of ideas. But there is something in the system, in the filmmaking culture, which is encouraging this creativity – or productivity.

Which suggests that if you look around and see that many of the best filmmakers here and now have only made a handful of British films, then perhaps there is something wrong, not with them, but with the filmmaking culture.

The specific films that directors have tried to make, and failed to make, are perhaps the simplest, easiest to recognise examples of unmade films – examples of the dark matter of British independent cinema. But there is far more dark matter out there. There are all the films that you think of, that you dream of, but which you know are not possible within the landscape you are working in. This can be for a multitude of reasons that attach themselves to one particular idea or project – the potential budget is too large, the story too small, there are no stars, the genre is wrong… or it doesn't fit any particular genre.

But in a way, the specific reasons for why one individual film does not get made is not the point. What is more pertinent is the way the system functions. There are broader gravitational forces at work.

Many filmmakers who have started making films in Britain, subsequently look to America – think of Lynne Ramsay, Andrea Arnold, Andrew Haigh, Danny Boyle, Stephen Daldry, Christopher Nolan, James Marsh. Or they find it easier to work in television, commercials, or theatre, or they decide to make studio films. For an individual director this may be a choice they are happy to make.

But it leaves British independent cinema sadly depleted. Think of the films that we have missed out on. If the environment allowed, or encouraged, British filmmakers who have already been successful, as everyone in this book has been, to carry on making the films they want to make, here in Britain, they wouldn't need to be as productive as Bergman or Godard to transform the landscape of British cinema. Even if filmmakers were only making one film every two years, we would now have ten films made here in Britain by Lynne Ramsay, instead of two; ten British films by Jonathan Glazer, instead of two; eleven films made here in Britain by Paweł Pawlikowski, instead of three; ten by Stephen Daldry, instead of three; six by Steve McQueen, instead of one. And so on.

Who knows what those films would have been? But surely British cinema would be richer if they had been made. This is the real dark matter. The films that these directors might have made.

Maybe it is the volume of this dark matter – the number of the unmade films – that explains why, as you look around the landscape of British independent cinema, it resembles an abandoned building site, with roads mapped out, foundations dug, random piles of bricks here and there, bags of cement and sand lying around unused, and only an occasional building standing... unoccupied, looking lonely in the surrounding chaotic landscape.

INTERVIEWS

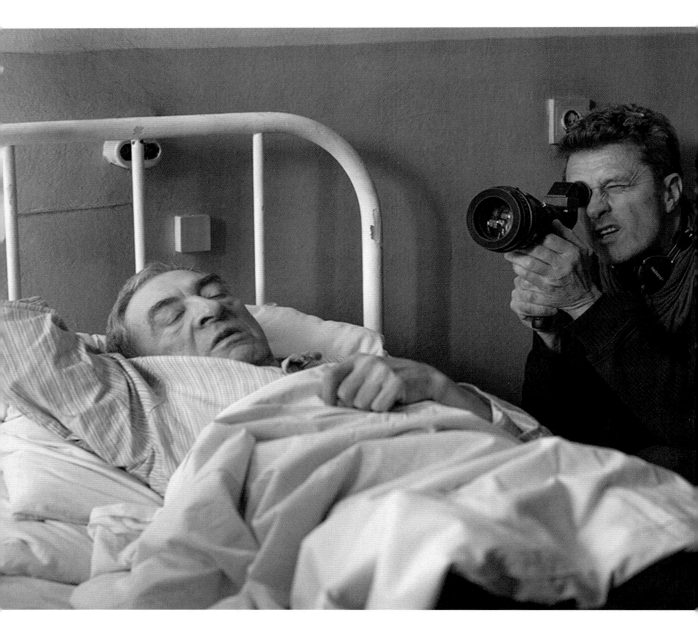

Paweł Pawlikowski, on set, *Ida* (2013). (photo: Sylwester Kazmierczak)

Paweł Pawlikowski

The last time I met Paweł was at the Sarajevo Film Festival about five years ago. At one point, many years earlier, we tried to get Paweł to make a film through Revolution Films, but unfortunately it never happened. These are excerpts from a conversation that took place on 25 April, 2020.

MW In your email you said you look back at your time at the BBC as a sort of golden age for you…

PP Yes. You could go to lunch with a commissioning editor, just write an idea down on a serviette and get very drunk and then enthusiastically have it signed off and go and shoot it. So it was kind of ideal. As long as you had ideas, of course. I ran out of ideas at some point.

It's good to be an institutional rebel, which is what I was at the time, you know. Going against the grain and getting paid.

MW Your documentaries were for *Arena* [a BBC documentary strand]?

PP I did one with *Arena*, but they tended to be for *Bookmark*, which was nominally a literary programme. But I just used the literature as a starting point. I made a road movie through Europe with a tram driver from Leningrad who happened to be Dostoevsky's great-grandson; or, one about the siege of Sarajevo and the oral epic poetry of the

Serbs. Nobody watched *Bookmark* much, so you had a lot of freedom to try things out. The editor was the novelist Nigel Williams, a very nice man and now a good friend. He gave me my break.

MW   It feels like a lot of the people I have been talking to, find that avoiding the development process helps.

PP   For documentaries it's a much more of an improvised adventure. You jump in and then you think on your feet. With feature films it doesn't quite work like that. It's just so much more complicated to create a world that isn't there to start with. It's also more difficult because I've become much more demanding of myself, I suppose. I was a bit of an amateur when I was making those docs – more or less between '89 and '95 – which was a really interesting time, with Eastern Europe opening up. When I moved to fiction it became a more tortured affair… coming up with a story that I really wanted to tell. How do you keep it alive? How do you avoid being hostage to bad literature? Which most scripts are.

I remember the first fictional film I made – *The Stringer* – I had a script, which I became the victim of… though I had written it. British Screen put some money into the film, and the BBC, and Polish TV. The budget was a million and a half. I went to film in Russia, and when I was in Russia I realised that the world there is just so much more interesting than my bloody script. My instinct was just to run away, or to rewrite the thing, but they wouldn't let me.

After that I made a low-budget film with my friend Ian Duncan, based on five pages of script, so we wouldn't be hostages to bad literature. We got a documentary budget from the BBC. We shot chronologically. We took a little break in the middle to edit and rethink. A kind of organic film.

MW   And that was *Twockers*? It was financed by the BBC?

PP   It was made for BBC Documentaries. It was done very cheaply, which gave us freedom. We shot with a very small crew. Available light. And we wanted it to be very photographic. Unlike the run-of-the-mill social drama. That was a really good learning experience for me, but the BBC shelved it. They'd just got bollocked in the press for making a documentary with faked-up scenes, so they got really nervous about this little fiction, which felt like reality. *Twockers* was a kind of rehearsal for *Last Resort*, which I did next.

MW   Do you see working in TV and cinema as the same thing?

PP   At the time, yes. Cinema is what I grew up on and really loved, but when I started making films it was for TV and I didn't think it was a problem. The main criterion was freedom. I wanted to be free to do this thing that I realised I do quite well: inventing a story that meant something; finding actors, locations, and trying things out – this way or that – constantly writing and rewriting to find a shape that felt right and scenes that lived and breathed and sometimes had poetry and didn't smell of screenwriting.

MW   We do some films which are improvised, but financiers often seem to think this is a sort of trick, to get their money sooner rather than later.

PP   Well, I don't think my films are improvised. Maybe in the very early ones there was some improv on set, but it was all from material prepared in advance. There are so few actors who can improvise well. Most of the time you just end up with clichés. Another reason I stopped doing loose improvisation is that I try to tell stories visually, in strong images, which is hard to do if there's too much freedom. So it's more about a kind of open, sculpting process.

So with *Last Resort*, it was a twenty-page story, with some scenes written out, and I went to Ruth Caleb at the BBC, who was into low-budget stuff. I think our budget was just under £300k. We had a tiny crew, with just one electrician and one camera assistant/clapper loader. In the script I merged two stories I'd been playing with for a while. One about a woman coming to England from Eastern Europe with her son, whose new English husband doesn't turn up at the airport. The other was about people living in this dead-end seaside town, this Costa del Dole, where asylum-seekers get dumped and can't leave. I spent a lot of time in Margate, meeting locals and refugees, and taking a lot of pictures. And then we started shooting, more or less chronologically. Sometimes the weather or situation gave me an idea for a completely different scene, so I just went off and shot that. I knew Margate like the back of my hand. And then we had a three-week break, more or less like I used to have when making docs, so I could see what worked, what didn't, and re-write the rest accordingly. I mean I always knew the beginning, middle and end and what the story was about, but I didn't always know how to get there without the boring scenes that just get you from A to B and explain stuff.

MW It was all BBC money?

PP Entirely. I had this genius line producer, Chris Collins, an unsung hero of low-budget British filmmaking, who performed miracles with the budget. Then Lizzie Francke saw it and invited it to Edinburgh and from there it went to Sundance.

MW It was quite a few years before you then made *My Summer of Love* and those are your only two films set in England. Why?

PP There are several reasons. One is possibly that I just don't have that many stories to tell in England. All I could come up with were foreigners or misfit teenagers. I was much more drawn towards Eastern Europe, the world I grew up in and left, and where I made my documentaries.

MW You talked to Andrew [Eaton] about doing a film at Revolution – something about bringing circus animals across...

PP Mongolia. Yeah... that was a crazy idea about a wolf trainer I met in Mongolia. It was going to be a kind of road movie in a train carriage. This beautiful man, Amgalan was his name, had his own railway carriage for going on tours, in which he built compartments for his performing animals – among them, wolves. And when he went on tour he would attach this carriage to different trains, and criss-cross the lands with his wife and young niece who was a contortionist. He belonged to a dying world and the film had a melancholy ending. It was a hybrid of documentary and fiction. From a logistical point of view, a total nightmare. Just imagine trains, Mongolia, Russia, wolves, yaks, borders, permissions. We needed at least $1,000,000.

MW Was that a project where you lost interest in it – or was it simply the money didn't come?

PP The money didn't come and without a serious backer it seemed hopeless – and the BBC weren't interested. But I don't know, maybe if I'd dug in, like one of these fanatical Russian directors who spend seven years making one film, maybe I could have pulled it off.

I also spent a few years on another idea, something set in the Thames Estuary, which I love – a kind of road movie on a clapped out sailing boat, but again, very difficult to make. Everything on water is difficult to make. So... I might still do it one day, but it just felt like: 'God it's going to be heavy lifting, I'm going to spend years on this, and I have a wife and kids.' In the end, I can't blame the investors. If you really, really want to do something, you usually can do it.

MW You co-write a lot of your stuff, but often with different writers?

PP Yeah. But I realise now that I'm the one who invents the thing, so most writers end up being very frustrated. The script is just a means to an end and the re-writing never stops, not even while we're filming. In the end, there's only one author, the person who is there at the beginning and at the end, whose taste and feeling is decisive, who finds the tone, who says 'yes' to this and 'no' to that. And who takes responsibility for the whole thing when it fails. As you can imagine, most British screenwriters, who mainly come from the theatre, hate my guts.

MW   Were there other projects before *My Summer of Love*?

PP   I got a lot of projects sent to me after *Last Resort*. Among them was a film about Sylvia Plath and Ted Hughes. I thought, 'God, what a love story!' It reminded me a bit of the disastrous relationship of my parents. But there was already a script, so I said, 'I'd love to get involved, as long as you allow me to mess with the story in order to find the film.' The script was of the biopic variety, where one thing leads to another and lives are explained in terms of cause and effect.

We had to cast up, in order to find the money and Gwyneth Paltrow was one of the contenders who would make it financeable. I met Gwyneth Paltrow and I liked her for the part. There were some aspects of Sylvia about her, and about her relationship with her father and mother, so there was something to build on. Then I met a lot of male actors for Ted Hughes. Daniel Day-Lewis didn't want to do it. Everyone else didn't feel right. And then, one of the American investors read the original script and decided wow, this is genius! Don't mess with this text. So I was stuck with a script that I didn't like, with executives who had opinions, an Oscar-winning star with a busy schedule and no time to mess around. And no one convincing as Ted Hughes. I jumped off, in the nick of time.[*]

---

[*]   *Sylvia* (2003) was subsequently directed by Christine Jeffs, with Daniel Craig as Hughes.

But I was up for a big love story, and this is where I came across Helen Cross's book *My Summer of Love*. I liked the relationship between the two girls at the centre of it. There was quite a lot of other stuff – the miners' strike, the Yorkshire Ripper, a pubful of characters and a murder – which I got rid of. Then I added a third character based on an evangelist priest I'd once met and wanted to make a documentary about. The priest had wanted to put up a 20-metre cross on top of Pendle Hill in Lancashire, which he claimed was still haunted by witches. So I had an ambition to shoot this Cecil B. DeMille number with thousands of people carrying a huge cross and tell their stories around that. But then the priest didn't get the planning permission from the local council and just gave up. So I put him and the cross into *My Summer of Love*.

Anyway we started shooting... and again, we shot some good scenes. An interesting film was starting to emerge, but it became clear that some of the scenes ahead, and some of the plotting were not up to the mark. So I stopped filming after three weeks and took a break. But we hadn't budgeted for the break, so then the three-week break became a two-month break while Chris and Tanya tried to find some more money. I rewrote the second half substantially, without changing the ending. And then we went back to West Yorkshire and shot the rest. Thank God that summer turned out to be the summer of the century and we got away with it. I don't think that a hiatus is an expensive luxury. Not if you build it into the schedule. The biggest waste of money is making a bad film, sticking to a bad script, with people looking away and pretending it's working. *My Summer of Love* actually made money.

MW The next film you made was in France. In Paris. *The Woman in the Fifth*. Did France seem somewhere more cinematic to you, in some way?

My Summer of Love (2004). (© Take Partnership/Apocalypso Pictures)

PP I hadn't made a film for five years. I was a single parent, looking after my kids and teaching at film school. I was stuck in Oxford, because their school was in Oxford. Then they went to university and Paris seemed like a cool place to escape to. These very nice producers from Haut et Court sent me a book by Douglas Kennedy,* who writes best-selling airport novels. And they said: 'We know this one doesn't really add up, but it's got atmosphere, so you can go and do whatever you

---

*   *The Woman in the Fifth*

want with it.' So… I'm just, retrospectively, trying to understand why the fuck did I do it? I guess it sounded like a good idea to get away from myself and make something that had nothing to do with me. I really liked Ethan Hawke and thought it might be something for him. But when I started adapting the novel, I realized that I'm not really into thrillers, even the metaphysical ones, so I got rid of most the murders and the police procedure and turned it into some kind of an opaque psychodrama. Something about guilt, schizophrenia and suicide. Possibly, I didn't get away from the novel enough, so it became this strange hybrid, not just in terms of genre, but also in terms of cultural identity. It had an American writer in Paris, which is a kind of familiar cliché, it had a Polish waitress, it had Kristin Scott Thomas, who plays a strange Hungarian, who possibly is not alive. The crew were French, my DoP [Director of Photography] was Polish, the key actress English and the key actor American. I didn't see any problem with that until I saw the film when it was finished. I'm actually very fond of this film, but judging by most people's reactions, it doesn't work.

MW   Did you go to Poland to make *Ida*, or did you go to Poland for personal reasons and then start making films in Poland?

PP   It's difficult to say, you know, the chicken and egg. I think officially I went to shoot the film, but after months of scouting, casting and just being there, I felt very much back home.

MW   Was *Ida* financed from the UK?

PP   The money came from Poland, UK and Denmark, but it was a 100% Polish film.

It seemed like a really uncommercial, hopeless idea – black and white, static camera, Polish dialogue, about a nun. I played with this story for years and then brought it to an English producer,

Eric Abrahams, who gave me some money to go and develop it, which is what I did. And then the British playwright Rebecca Lenkiewicz joined, as a co-writer. I started casting and looking for locations, but Eric's people took the project to Cannes to try and pre-sell it – no one was interested. So *Ida* seemed to be dead in the water. But then Ewa [Puszczyńska], the Polish producer, said: 'We've done all this work, why don't we just start shooting, and see what happens? We have half the budget from the Polish Film Institute, why not just start and see what happens.' So we started filming, while rest of the money came in dribs and drabs. There was definitely no money for my usual hiatus, which was a problem because, again, the second half of the story was creaky and full of clunky scenes. But then snow fell early, paralysing the country and we stopped filming ten days from the end. Very lucky for me. I got my break to reshape the script and invent new scenes and Ewa to raise some extra money. And the final ten days – after the break – were like a home run.

MW   Your two British films were very successful at festivals, but I was wondering whether you feel that making a successful Polish film had a different impact than making a successful British film? Whether the cultural space for a Polish film was… better than for the *Last Resort* or *My Summer of Love*?

PP   On the contrary, Polish films didn't exist at festivals at all, not since Kieślowski in the early Nineties. For Cannes, Poland didn't count. *Ida* got passed over by Venice. So there was nothing strategic about making a Polish film. And most of my friends thought I was committing professional suicide. Why a black-and-white film in Polish about a nun with a bunch of unknowns, if you could be working with well-known actors in English, on a proper budget? But it felt good to me. I felt I landed on firm ground. The landscapes, the people, the history, the pop songs, the jazz, the Sixties – it felt close and familiar. It was my childhood. I knew that world. I knew how to do this.

MW Then there was *Cold War*. Also produced by Ewa.

PP Yes. Ewa in tandem with Tanya [Seghatchian], who produced *My Summer of Love* – an old friend and ally. The financing was complicated and we had ten different locations in three countries and a script that kept changing. But Ewa and Tanya kept the show on the road and left me space to do things my way.

MW Are you preparing a new film?

PP Not in any concrete way. I'm mainly writing. One story, which I've almost finished, is set during the Warsaw Uprising. It's expensive and pretty 'feel bad', so it's hard to imagine it getting financed in the current climate. But it was good – therapeutic – to write it. I'm also co-writing a TV series about a woman spy, set between 1930 and 1950, in Weimar, Shanghai, Moscow, Geneva, Oxford, East Berlin. I have to say it's so much more relaxing to be just the writer. Not to worry about the film and feel responsible for what ends up on the screen. If the cinema doesn't come back, I'll probably end up doing this full time. And live longer.

Filmography

1998 *The Stringer*
1998 *Twockers* (TV)
2000 *Last Resort*
2004 *My Summer of Love*
2011 *The Woman in the Fifth* (France)
2013 *Ida* (Poland)
2018 *Cold War* (Poland)

Danny Boyle

I have only met Danny once or twice, but there are several people that we have both worked with, like the production designers Mark Tildesley and Mark Digby, the cinematographer Alwin Kuchler, and the writer Frank Cottrell-Boyce. These are excerpts from a conversation that took place on 29 April 2020.

DB When I got your email I started thinking about all the failed projects – we shouldn't call them that, because you don't want to stigmatise them – and wondering how many might end up on television, because there's one of mine I was going to talk to you about that we're now trying to make as television.

MW What is that?

DB That's *Ingenious Pain*. Have you ever read it?

MW No.

DB It's by Andrew Miller. He's an amazing writer. He's sort of hidden behind Ian McEwan and Martin Amis. But he is a great writer. His first book was *Ingenious Pain*, which has got this extraordinary idea in it, of a child... who feels no pain. Which is very dangerous. It's a romance, of course. He uses it as a metaphor for romantic love. He becomes a surgeon because his not feeling pain helps him. It is set in the eight-

Danny Boyle on set, *28 Days Later* (2002). (© 20th Century Fox/Courtesy Everett Collection/Mary Evans)

eenth century. It's a wonderful book – Patrick Marber was trying to adapt it into a film. But it's got an extraordinary idea at the end of it that we could never get to work. And I was thinking about that moment, where you decide internally that it doesn't work, that moment where it falls, the tipping point that these projects have. And it's really arbitrary,

I think, because you think about some of the stuff you've made, and you think, 'Well, that didn't really work,' but we all believed it would and we ploughed on, whereas this, we decided it wouldn't work.

I'm not really a writer but I had a go at adapting it – that's how stuck we were. And Patrick's now trying to adapt it into a television format, which may well suit it better. A much more discursive format.

Then there was a Solomon Grundy project and then there is one that Frank and I were working on – a Bowie project. *Ingenious Pain* and the Bowie project are both about five years old. Whereas *Solomon Grundy* is… fuck, fifteen years old.

Solomon Grundy's based on, obviously, the nursery rhyme, though apparently he's a Marvel character as well. Because they've just aggrandised everything into the Marvel Universe. But anyway it's based on the old British nursery rhyme. I was approached about it fifteen years ago. It was a finished script by a wonderful writer, Robert Jacobs, and it was utterly captivating.

It was the seven ages of man, really, told through seven days. It was just one of those grand projects that's rooted in a very specific character. It was based on a British novel by a guy called Dan Gooch, but they had moved the story to America. And rightly, I thought. America has that sense that you can get lost there in such a huge space. It felt like a more comfortable place for the story.

So we set about working on it. We worked on a draft for many, many years. The big question was about the central character? How could you make him the same person. It felt like there would be a technical solution to the problem, and we got to the point of trying to map Jake Gyllenhaal's face onto different bodies.

And then *Benjamin Button* was announced, which was a film that was going to use a huge amount of technology, and take an even more extraordinary story, but a similar principle in the sense of a lifetime told in a very unusual way. And so we were kind of shunted off to the sidelines. So our tipping point was decided for us by the market – by 'everybody's going to want to be watching *Benjamin Button*'. There was never a moment where we went: 'Yeah, let's close the page on that one.' There was only the moment, many months after, when you realise: 'Oh, we're no longer talking about that project anymore.' So it had died.

Bizarrely, I think you can see the influence of that idea in *Slumdog Millionaire* – which is a life story in chapters, albeit one that finishes when he's still in his twenties. But still a life story, really. Even though Simon Beaufoy, who wrote *Slumdog*, was never involved in *Solomon Grundy*.

Ironically *Slumdog Millionaire* ended up at the Academy Awards the same year as *Benjamin Button*. In fact we benefited from people being more interested in our film than they were in *Benjamin Button*, which should have taught me something about the Solomon Grundy idea, but it hasn't, because – even more ironically – the day after you sent your email a script arrived here, sent by one of the young British producers on *Yesterday*, the Richard Curtis film that I made with Working Title. It's by an Irish writer and it is the same idea, but told over 24 hours rather than 7 days. It is very attractive. The bug hasn't died. I know you are planning a project as well. So obviously it's out there, that idea.

MW When you say 'we' were working on *Solomon Grundy*, who is the 'we'? You and a producer?

DB It was after I had done *Trainspotting* and it was sent to me by an American producer called Richard Gladstein. After *Trainspotting* I was sent stuff. At one point I was going to do *Alien 4*, before I realised that I would be hopelessly lost doing a film like that. This was another project that I got sent.

MW I made a TV film in the early Nineties, in Belfast for BBC Northern Ireland. Robert Cooper was running the drama department there. He had taken over from you, I think.

DB I'm really from the theatre. I grew up in the theatre. Although my secret passion was always films. And this job was being advertised to produce TV drama in Belfast. For various political reasons they wouldn't make an internal appointment of somebody from Northern Ireland. They wanted an outsider

And I applied and I was told that nobody else applied. So I got the job. When I got there I said I'd commission writers I had worked with in the theatre. I said, 'I'm also going to direct these films.' And they went, 'Oh no. Producers don't direct.' And I said, 'Well, I am going to. But you only have to pay me one salary.'

So that was my start. It was a wonderful time.

MW The perfect environment. You have the ability to dream up ideas, get people to write them, and then make them.

DB Yes.

MW You've been working in TV again recently. I was wondering how you would compare now to then?

DB When I started it was at the end of a glorious time for BBC's drama output. I came at the fag end of that. It was beginning to die. But it had been structurally significant in our society. My experience as a kid, growing up, seeing those BBC dramas, was hugely significant for me. I benefited from that.

MW It seems to me that the sort of space there was then to make stories about the detail of people's lives as they live them in Britain, doesn't really exist anymore in television, but it has never really existed in British cinema. It seems to me that in America you can make a small story set in a suburb or set in a small town, and it can be cinema. But, not here in Britain. I was wondering whether, when you shifted to cinema, that you felt you had to shift the story you were telling?

DB I think at the time you were doing *Family* [a series written by Roddy Doyle]. I did this thing called *Mr. Wroe's Virgins*, in Manchester, which was a wonderful book by this Lancashire writer, Jane Rogers. And I managed to attract Jonathan Pryce to do it, which gave it status. And I then got a couple of episodes of *Inspector Morse*. And the crew would work on *Morse* for half a year, doing four or six episodes, or whatever, and then the rest of the year they would work on a Spielberg project, like *Raiders*, or one of those big movies. So I had this exposure, as a relatively young guy, to film-crew aesthetics, their standards. That was a huge help. I only realised those things in retrospect. How important it was working on *Morse*, or with an actor like Jonathan Pryce.

Then I got sent the script of *Shallow Grave*. Andrew Macdonald and John Hodge were looking for a director. They'd developed it with Film4, and Film4 sent them off to find a director. And I was the least unsuitable… so I got the gig.

MW There was then a whole phase of you and Andrew Macdonald and John Hodge working together. How did that work? Did you sit together and collectively work out what your next project was?

DB Some of my principles about the way I work come from theatre. I trained at the Royal Court Theatre where it's very collaborative. But it's also very writer led. So I was very keen to work in a cooperative way – the three of us working together.

So we did *Shallow Grave*. It did quite well and we said: 'Well, we should do another one.' And a friend of Andrew had given him this book, *Trainspotting*, and he gave it to us both. I've still got my copy of it. And that was a turning point for me on a personal level. In terms of the ambition of what you can do in Britain. The novel had this fury and linguistic verve. It was hugely ambitious. So we tried to reflect that in the film. And we had a good jumping-off point, having made a film together that had worked… we got on reasonably well, we cast it in an interesting way, and Ewan McGregor had a bit of presence, so suddenly that gave us a bit of a lift.

I think a lot of people felt that the film was going to be an unwatchable drug film, which they usually are… pretty unwatchable. They mean more to the creators than anybody who has to actually watch the thing. So we basically got a free hand if we kept the budget to two million quid. We could do what we wanted.

MW Was that all Film4 money? And PolyGram?

DB PolyGram had picked up *Shallow Grave*, and done very nicely out of it. They were in that period of a very bullish expansion, which we both benefited from, I think. They wanted to distribute films like they were big films that anybody would go and see on a Friday night.

MW In this first phase of making films, you're effectively making one film a year.

DB I think because the first two films we made were successful, financially, they gave us the freedom to do what we wanted. Or we thought it gave us freedom, and so we did do what we wanted. Then we hit the buffers on a few things and you have to learn a different kind of discipline, which is more applicable to most people, which is to have a couple of ideas to see which one will go.

But for a while we would just announce what we wanted to do. A mate of mine gave me the Alex Garland book, *The Beach*. We just said, 'Let's do this.' That allows you to work quickly, because you don't have that development period where you're developing a number of projects. We were doing one thing at a time, and each thing that we decided on, we were fully committed to.

Before *The Beach* we did *A Life Less Ordinary*, which was very unsuccessful, but we absolutely committed to John's script and we just went off and did it. The same with *The Beach*. And then it all fell apart a bit, really, after that. We all kind of got separated.

MW Why did that happen? You were incredibly successful, making your films, British films, but at the same time big international films. They weren't confined by any sense of budget, or sense of ambition. It seems like the perfect environment. What made you decide, collectively, to go your separate ways?

DB *The Beach* was very traumatic because the scale was massive. Was huge. We decided we were going to have Leo, and so the budget became enormous. And the reception of it was very mixed. It fractured us really.

I went back to television, because I wanted that freedom. I did a couple of bizarre Jim Cartwright pieces, which I really enjoyed doing. And it was sort of an experiment, for me, in a way – stepping away from Andrew and John, I suppose. Because they went off to make their own film, *Final Curtain*, with Peter O'Toole, I think. I remember reading about that in the paper and being very hurt. Meanwhile, of course, I was doing what I wanted to do. So I can hardly claim to be an innocent victim.

And then Alex wrote this script, *28 Days Later*, and we got back together.

So it was very quick working. You're lucky if your taste is such that you are interested in projects that interest the financiers. Or you've had enough success that you're not thought of as too great a risk. Also, I like working quite cheaply – and obviously Andrew's a brilliant producer at raising money. That has to be said as well.

I'd worked with this cinematographer Anthony Dod Mantle on the TV shows because I had seen his work on Dogme films. I've never been that interested in the aesthetic of cinematography, I've always been more interested in camera operation. That relationship between the operator and the actors, and the camera is the dynamic of your film.

So, we brought Anthony Dod Mantle onto *28 Days* and we worked with these little digital cameras and I'm very proud of that because it was the first real mainstream, big release of a film that was made with these domestic cameras.

MW So then you're still with Andrew, but with Alex Garland rather than John Hodge writing the scripts.

DB That's right.

MW Were you formally part of DNA?

DB No, and when I look back on that, Michael, I think, 'Wow'. Because I remember – this sounds terribly glamorous, and I hate saying things like this – but I remember being in a car on the way to the Cannes Film Festival where we were showing *Trainspotting* out of competition. I remember being in the back of the car and Andrew saying to me, 'I'm setting up a company called DNA', and I remember thinking, 'Oh, probably that will be Danny and Andrew', and he said, 'No, it's Duncan and Andrew.' And I was kind of… you know, I'm never one to… So I said, 'Okay', and I didn't really do anything about it. And that was a seed, really. You know Andrew's grandfather was Emeric Pressburger, who was often overshadowed by Michael Powell's reputation, and I think Andrew still carried that feeling of, 'I do all the work, and directors take all the credit'. It's not quite true, but there is some truth in that, as we all know. It's just the way the business moves and swerves.

MW You were still together on *28 Days Later* and on *Sunshine*. I remember on *Sunshine*, me and Andrew [Eaton] tried to persuade you and Andrew [Macdonald] to let us come and shoot with Steve Coogan at night, on your set.

DB I thought that was a brilliant idea, but I remember Andrew being very nervous about the whole prospect. Partly because of the damage to the sets that he thought you might do. But I thought, 'That's a brilliant idea'. You were going to shoot through the night, weren't you?

MW Yes.

DB We were going to shoot through the day and you'd turn up at night, get the sets for free, and I thought, provided we could release the film first that would be fine.

MW We thought it was going to happen for a while.

DB The set was brilliantly designed, of course, by Mark Tildesley, who I had seen doing your work, and then met him to do *28 Days Later*. It's like you kind of like cross-pollinate. Did you see that Irfan [Khan] died today?

MW Yes.

DB I remember seeing him in *A Mighty Heart* and then he was in *Slumdog*.

MW So was *Sunshine* the last one where you worked with Andrew?

DB Yes. After *28 Days Later* I went off to do *Millions*. Graham Broadbent sent me Frank's [Cottrell-Boyce] script and I'd always loved Frank's work so I went off to make that while Alex was writing *Sunshine*. It took a long time, *Sunshine*. You haven't done your space movie yet, have you?

MW No, because I couldn't get on your set. The only way I could afford to do a space movie would be on someone else's set.

DB Wait until you have a go at a space movie, you'll see what I mean. That took a long, long time. Space movies are fucking difficult. It is a closed environment, in a way that you can't appreciate until you do it. You end up dominating in a way that excludes your partners. I think after *Sunshine* Alex and Andrew both wanted to work with a different director, and I'd found it tough as well. Then Christian

Sunshine (1994). (© Twentieth Century Fox Film Corporation/Dune Entertainment LLC/ TCF Hungary Film Rights Exploitation Limited Liability Company)

Colson sent me Simon Beaufoy's script, *Slumdog Millionaire,* and I remember asking Andrew if he wanted to come in on it. So obviously we were still talking to each other, so it wasn't toys out of the pram, or anything like that.

I think Alex and I had very different philosophical approaches to *Sunshine.* Alex has very much a hard atheistic philosophy and I'm a bit more spiritual. We sort of fell out over that. So he then went through a couple of different directors, and then he ended up directing himself.

MW I was going to say it must have been a complicating factor if Alex wanted to direct himself?

DB I think he probably did. But he didn't realise until he'd tried a couple of other directors and found us all too annoying

MW And since then you've been working with Christian Colson. Do you develop stuff together?

DB Yes. That brings us back to *Ingenious Pain*. Patrick is a friend of Christian. That project came through Patrick and Christian's friendship.

Frank's script about Bowie in Berlin, *Always Crashing in the Same Car*, was something that Christian and I commissioned. I need a producer to work with, I've realised that. I love the relationship with writers, but I also need the relationship with a producer. I'm not a producer, Michael, in any coherent sense of the word.

I get a producer credit these days, but it's just to sort of have voting rights.

MW Do you have a company together?

DB No. It's probably influenced by Andrew Macdonald and his DNA decision, but I've always remained slightly separate from companies. Christian has his own company. I tend to do things on a shake of a hand rather than with contracts and things like that really.

I still feel very committed to *Ingenious Pain*, and the Bowie script – to those bits of dark matter.

MW What happened with the Bowie script?

DB Well obviously you need the music because I didn't want to make a *Velvet Goldmine* or anything like that. It's about the relationship between Bowie and Iggy in Berlin. We sent it to Bowie and he didn't want to do it. He just wasn't interested in it.

Steve Jobs (2015). (© Universal Studios/Legendary Pictures)

At the time it was like, 'Oh well, what a shame'. It felt arbitrary, but after I understood that he didn't want to have anything about the past because he was working on new material.

MW Recently you have been working again in television with *Babylon* and *Trust*. What was the pull back into TV? Were they projects you developed?

DB *Babylon* was my idea and we approached Jesse Armstrong and Sam Bain to write it. *Trust* was very much Christian's baby.

MW You have also worked in America but I get the sense that they are still, in essence, your films, British films, even though they were set in America. I assume you originated *127 Hours* from the UK. Was that the same with *Jobs* as well?

DB *Jobs* was Scott Rudin, you know. It's Rudin's baby and obviously he'd fallen out with Fincher. I don't know why. But, that was just a glorious script. I'm a lover of writers and just to have a go at that was a wonderful opportunity.

127 Hours was very much François Ivernel. That was dark matter for a while. Because I remember meeting Aron Ralston five, six years before we made it, and not being able to agree. I was very frustrated because I had a very clear idea of how I wanted to do the film, but he couldn't see what I wanted to do with it, so it went away. Then it came back after the success of *Slumdog*. That was one of those moments where you can get financing for a film about a man who cuts his arm off. I wrote that, and then Christian got Simon to improve the writing, but I wrote the structure.

That's dark matter that did crystallise ultimately and become a film.

Filmography

1994	*Shallow Grave*	2008	*Slumdog Millionaire*
1996	*Trainspotting*	2010	*127 Hours*
1997	*A Life Less Ordinary*	2013	*Trance*
2000	*The Beach*	2014	*Babylon* (TV Mini-Series, 1 episode)
2001	*Strumpet* (TV)		
2001	*Vacuuming Completely Nude in Paradise* (TV)	2015	*Steve Jobs* (US film)
		2017	*T2 Trainspotting*
2002	*28 Days Later...*	2018	*Trust* (TV Series, 3 episodes)
2004	*Millions*	2019	*Yesterday*
2007	*Sunshine*		

Joanna Hogg

These are excerpts from a conversation that took place on 15 April 2020.

MW   Are you in London?

JH   I'm in Shoreditch which is normally so noisy, and it's so quiet you can hear the birds, and the air's really fresh. It's very strange.

MW   Were you working on a production?

JH   We had started the sound mix but then my lovely sound designer got the virus – quite badly. I was really worried about him for a few days because he couldn't shake it off. Now fingers crossed he's on the mend, but I don't know when he's going to be ready to get back to work.

MW   The film is due out this year or next year?

JH   I was hoping it was going to be this year but now all the festivals are being cancelled.

MW   We had a film, which was supposed to show in Tribeca, and then be released in America in May. Tribeca was cancelled and now it is just getting an online release.

JH   But in a funny way you'll probably get a bigger online audience than in normal times.

MW It seems like, since your first film, you've been pretty successful in getting stuff made. Are you able now to make pretty much what you want, when you want?

JH It's funny because I always use you as my benchmark for whether I'm prolific or not. I'm never prolific enough compared to you! I think I'm very slow but I'm trying to speed up a bit. That's partly because I conceived of a project [*The Souvenir*] that was two films, which I had wanted to shoot back-to-back. And we started pre-production planning to shoot two films, going from one to the other, and I really wanted that because I thought someone's going to stop me from shooting the second one. I was convinced that the first one would come out and... Anyway, it was a miracle that we managed to get the second one made, two years later. I shot the first in summer 2017 and the second in 2019. I think from the outside that seems very fast, because of how slow it is usually to get a film out and into the world.

MW You work with a small team of regular collaborators on set, is that true on the producing side as well?

JH Well, no. That's changed over the years. I made my first film with one producer who I didn't work with again. And then the next two were the same producer. And then that producer sadly died, and it made me think, okay, well how do I want to do things? Maybe I want to take things more into my own hands.

So then I set up a production company and produced the first *Souvenir* through that production company, and brought in a producer, because I wanted someone to deal with that side. But I found it quite a headache. I don't know how you find it, because you've got your own company and you have had for some time. But I find just being asked things about the budget... I don't have the spare brain cells to deal with it. I'm not interested in that side of it, I just want to get the film made. But I want total control!

So it all went okay, we made the film, but I found it quite a stress having this double role. Then for the second film the BBC said, 'You must get another company to work with you.' So I joined forces with Element Pictures, an Irish company, and they were totally sympathetic with what I was doing and wanted to work with me at some point anyway. It was something we had to do in order to satisfy the BBC and get the money

But, to answer your question, the producing side has never been as smooth as the other sides. I've worked with the same production designer, the same editor, the same sound designer, all these people are really precious to me. The DoP changed with *The Souvenir* because the guy who I wanted to shoot it had personal problems and he went to shoot a TV series, and I was thinking , 'Oh my god, one of my key people, what am I going to do?' It's like a marriage breakup, or something. I find it really terrifying. But in the end I survived. I mean you always think it's all going to be different, but I still managed to do what I wanted.

So on the creative side it's pretty consistent. But on the producing side I've always had challenges. I think I naturally want to fight the producer, and also myself at some point. I don't know, there's some authority thing or something... I don't know what it is.

MW   Having set up your company to make your films, don't you find it hard to finance the company from the budgets for your films? What size budget were you at with *The Souvenir*?

JH   The second part [of *The Souvenir*] was nearly £3 million – which is big money for me. The first one was two-and-a-half, or something. The previous films had been under a million, and I've always been

Joanna Hogg, with DoP David Raedeker, on set in Venice, *The Souvenir* (2019).
(photo: Agatha A. Nitecka/A24)

terrified of big budgets because I think 'OK, the more money you've got, the less control you have', so I like to keep them down.

    Archipelago was around a quarter of a million, maybe £300,000 after post-production. *Exhibition*, about £900,000.

MW And *Unrelated*? I saw a figure which was incredibly low, but I never trust it when you see incredibly low figures in articles. Knowing how expensive post-production houses are, it's hard to see how you hit some of these figures.

JH It really was tiny. To shoot it was something like £100,000, because it was a tiny crew and ever since I've tried to keep the crew really small. Most of the budget went on the rental of the house that the film was set in. And we shot on a Sony Z1, so it was really lo-fi, I mean it was as lo-fi as possible, hardly any lights to the distress of the cinematographer. People were on very low wage – all that deferral bollocks. And then in post-production I had an editor but they didn't work out and I thought 'OK, I'm going to do it, it's going to be easy' and it was really difficult. So I got in another editor, but it was really pretty much a one-man band. For a technophobe, I really got into the technology, we were cutting on Final Cut and I really understood the workflow. The problem is, technology changes so fast doesn't it?

But post-production was a nightmare until I found my editor who I've now worked with on every film since. I thought the film was going to be one of those vanity things that will never see the light of day.

MW How did you get it financed? Was the BFI involved?

JH No, there was no-one official involved, and that was partly by choice, not that they would have given me the money. But anyway, I just wanted to do it in a home-made way. I didn't want any interference from anybody. And it was thanks to the wonderful producer I had, Barbara Stone, who used to run the Gate Cinemas, with her husband. She found some of the money. I got £5,000 from my mum. It was really cobbled together.

MW And then did someone come in at post-production level to finish off the post-production?

JH Yes. I think £150,000 was the total figure. That's when I met Jovan, my lovely sound designer and we ended up making a 35 mm print of the film even though it was shot on the Sony Z1. It looks quite interesting.

MW We shot *In This World* on one of the very early Sonys – the PD150. The première was at Berlin, so it's a massive great screen. We thought it was going to look awful, but it was actually great, because there's so much texture. It was beautiful.

Did your mum get her money back?

JH   Well she didn't make a profit, put it that way.

MW   Right. From then on, starting with *Archipelago* were they all financed by the BBC and BFI?

JH   No. *Archipelago* was actually thanks to a Japanese investor. Gayle Griffiths saw *Unrelated* somewhere and said she would like to produce something with me. I was initially very suspicious. I think I told her about *Archipelago* and she said, 'Oh, I want to option it.' I've never liked the idea of someone else optioning your work because then they have rights over it. So I said, 'No, you can't option it.' So we worked something out where I kept the rights. And I liked her. She seemed very serious, and she turned out to be incredibly good and really rigorous in her approach. I really trusted her. She was an amazing organiser and loved working with people who she deemed to be creative. You don't get many producers like that – it wasn't about building a company and making lots of money. She always struggled financially because she put her heart and soul into the projects she worked on. I had the benefit of her amazing energy on *Archipelago* and then *Exhibition*. But on *Archipelago* none of those official funders were involved.

MW   *Exhibition* was the first time.

JH   Yes. We were in the system. And I was worried that I was suddenly going to be restricted by the BBC and the BFI. Because I don't work with a script. So no one sees what they're going to get.

MW   I always find there's a huge pressure from financiers for there to be a script. I wonder, do you think part of your success in getting stuff made recently is because you don't have a script? There's less ability for someone to mess you around for a year and half while they think about your script.

JH   Yeah, I guess it's designed to avoid that. But also, like you… I just love the energy. I love not quite knowing what's going to happen next. So

Archipelago (2010). (© Wild Horses Film Company)

I create a situation where I can change my mind, or invent as I go along. I think I just get my kicks out of taking risks and not knowing what's going to happen next. It's the energy you get from something being concocted in the moment that is so exciting.

MW   And by that point, because of your two first films, you were able to persuade the BFI and BBC that that's how you work and that's the end of it. If they wanted to be involved that's the way it goes.

JH   That's the way it goes. Somehow I managed to get it through, but then the budget was under a million – if it had been any more than I wouldn't have got away with it.

MW   On *The Souvenir*, the BBC and BFI funded the whole film on a story outline?

JH   Yeah. For a while It just seemed like we were going through mud, was it ever going to happen. Then Rose Garnett came on as head of BBC Film from Film4 and she really liked my films, and *The Souvenir* fell into her lap – thank god – and the energy really came from that – and she continues to be incredibly supportive. So these things that are partly luck. If Rose hadn't suddenly become head of BBC Film, I'm not sure whether it would have happened.

MW It was still quite a big gap before *The Souvenir*. Was that simply you thinking about what to do next?

JH It was partly that. *Exhibition* came out in 2013 and then I started thinking about *The Souvenir* a year later, maybe two. Thinking seriously in 2015. But it wasn't until 2017 that I shot it, so I don't know, time went by, it's a funny thing, because even though I don't write a script, I still spend a lot of time writing notes and preparing. A lot of that gets thrown out of the window once I start shooting because then there is a whole new energy. But somehow the work I do, even though no one sees it, it's the foundation of the film. So it's quite a slow build even though it seems like there's nothing there. It takes me time to find the next thing. Although right now even though I'm still in post [production] on *The Souvenir 2*, I'm trying to build the next thing. I want to step up the speed a bit.

MW I imagine from your first films that location was really important. I was curious to see you'd shot *The Souvenir* on a stage. How did you find that? I hate shooting on a stage I feel like the energy is so low... You were talking before about how the energy is in the moment with the actors and for me location is quite central to that. Was it because it was period that you chose to shoot on a stage or did you want to have more control visually?

JH One of the main reasons was that I wanted to recreate a flat that I lived in in the early Eighties. So I was never going to find that flat anywhere on location. And I thought, 'Oh well the Eighties is such a different time, everything looked so different, how am I going to get that feeling?' And then I started to think we've got to build it. And we looked all over the country for somewhere cheap enough and we ended up in West Raynham.

MW Near where I am now…

JH When I first saw it, I just fell in love with it. And so it was almost like we were shooting on location.

MW It's a very strange place; it's a very atmospheric place.

JH It is. When I first walked into that empty aircraft hangar, which at one end looks out onto the countryside, I just fell in love with that view. And then we built the flat and we treated it like very much like a location.

MW When you're working with a small crew, on location, it's quite easy to keep people in the location. When you're on stage people tend to break up and go and wander off.

JH Well there isn't much outside West Raynham, so there were no distractions. So actually I've come around to enjoying creating something inside a studio.

MW You said you were working on other projects?

JH There's one film which is set in Norfolk, funnily enough, that I want to do at some point but I'm still not quite ready to do it. It's not even a big project actually, it's just that for various reasons I'm not ready to do it. And I've got a project that would involve a lot more money, which worries me. Because in the end you're living in the real world and so you're trying to think about how to make things in the real world rather than in some fantasy world. If I want to make this project for £10 million, I can't believe I'm not going to have to show a script.

The Souvenir (2018). (© British Film Institute/BBC/The Souvenir Film Limited)

MW You went to film school, but you left film school 20 years before making your first film. In that phase, were there films that you were trying to get made?

JH Yes there were. My projects were incredibly ambitious when I came out of film school. One of them was like a James Bond film called *London, Paris, Rome.* It was absolutely a mega production. It was a complete fantasy, there was no way anyone was going to give me money to do that, so that was my mistake.

Then when I was directing TV stuff there were gaps and in those gaps I would think... Okay, well I'm going to brave it. I'm going to not do any more of this TV. When I go through old papers I've got quite a lot of scripts that never happened, scripts that never went anywhere, sort of ghost projects. I'd start developing something, but then of course the phone would ring and I would take the TV job. Partly for money, and I suppose it was partly confidence as well, because I hadn't made a film at that point. I'd been in TV so long it just got harder to get out of it.

MW   I get a sense that you don't particularly see a connection between that TV experience and what you do now, is that right? That was a different area of work completely?

JH   I did very soapy stuff.

MW   Right.

JH   Then finally I went 'I'm just going to do it.' I wanted no authority, I just wanted to do it completely in my own way. And I think Barbara helped me with that because she'd come from this experimental film landscape in New York in the Sixties, where you just pick up a camera and you're shooting the whole time. She had a very fluid idea of it, so her approach really helped free me up as well.

MW   It's interesting that your first few films weren't supported by those traditional routes that support the British film industry.

JH   I've never worked with script editors and I find them... I don't need a script editor, I don't want a script editor. I don't want to have to analyse in that way. I think the problem that young filmmakers have now is they have to go through those channels, whether it's a micro-budget scheme or whatever it is. There's script editors all over those projects to such a ridiculous degree. I think those films can't breathe.

Filmography

2007   *Unrelated*
2010   *Archipelago*
2013   *Exhibition*
2018   *The Souvenir*
2021   *The Souvenir: Part II* (completed but not yet released)

Asif Kapadia

I met Asif a long time ago at a screening of *The Warrior*. I was introduced to him by Tony Grisoni, a writer I had worked with on *In This World*, who had taught Asif at film school. That was the only time I had met him before the interview, but a few people who used to work at Revolution have been working with Asif and James Gay Reece's company, On the Corner. These are excerpts from a conversation that took place on 17 April 2020.

AK   I was thinking, before we were about to talk, that we have a lot of mutual friends. Like Tony [Grisoni] and Matt Whitecross who lives up the road. His kids go to the same school as mine. But we haven't really talked before.

MW   Yes, Matt's been working with you, hasn't he? You have a company with James which does a whole bunch of stuff besides your films?

AK   That's an interesting thing because we made a few films together, and it's grown. But actually running companies with people is quite complicated and political and challenging. So that company may well be coming to an end now, and I may well have to start my own thing, somewhere else. It's kind of a natural cycle – we start, we work together, do something that people like, we enjoy that – and then you

Asif Kapadia on set, *The Warrior* (2001). (Image courtesy Ronald Grant Archive/Mary Evans)

do it again, and you do it again, and then there are different issues going on. If you're a director it's really hard to be doing lots of things. Whereas when you're producing you can be producing lots of things. So he set up another company to do other stuff.

MW That's the sport stuff?

AK A lot of sports stuff, yeah. Which I got a bit bored with. I'm interested in making films, and I love sport, but I don't want to just bang out sport or have my name on stuff. That's where it's challenging running a company because so much of the time you're not actually being a director, you're just doing other stuff.

MW That is one of the things I wanted to ask people. What the key relationships are in getting stuff made? The producer is maybe the most important?

AK At the beginning, on *The Warrior* it was with Bertrand Faivre, a French producer, who really believed in me and gave me a chance to make my first feature. And we did a few things together, and then I would say, for whatever reason, that came to a natural closure – we were still friends, but we didn't work together. Then I went off and did some other stuff, and then I worked with James, and we made *Senna*. I was hired to make it. Then we did it again with *Amy*, and then we did it again with *Maradona*.

It was never my intention to be making documentaries. It was never a plan. So, somewhere along the way, the projects that didn't happen, kind of led me to do stuff where I could have a bit more control. The budgets were lower, I could change my mind, work the way I wanted to work, and it just so happened to be making movies out of archive. For me they are movies. Obviously they are seen by the outside world as docs. But they are constructed in such a way that they're trying to play like fiction. With docs I can do films that are not in English; I can do films about characters that are maybe not so lovable or likable; I can do interesting dark, twisted characters or stories, with not-happy endings – people die, you know. Which I found challenging in drama with development hell, and everything.

So that was what I was thinking when you contacted me: it's interesting how you change your path. Everything I studied, everything I was interested in, everything I wanted to do, I'm not doing. I've ended up doing something else. But I'd love to go back there.

MW Why is it hard to have the same freedom to tell a difficult story, or an unsympathetic story, in fiction? It doesn't seem like it should be.

AK I think it may have changed. The big thing for me was, post *The Warrior*, nobody from the UK said, 'Here, what do you want to do next? Here's some money.'

MW Why?

AK They never did. That's the funny thing. And for a time, you kind of keep it to yourself. I was hoping they'd say, 'We liked that film, it was kind of epic.' The film did quite well, but it didn't make loads of money at the box office. It was with Harvey [Weinstein] in America, so I had my Miramax experience of him, saying, 'If you don't sign a three-picture deal, we don't release the film.' And I said, 'I don't really want to do that. I really like doing one film at a time,' and he said, 'Well no one will ever see your movie.' I didn't sign, so he basically killed the film in America and a lot of international territories he owned it for.

That's the real world. You make a film, it won a couple of BAFTAs. Critically it did really well. Then I did another film called *Far North*, which is a mad film in the Arctic, and then it became a challenge to get the things I wanted to do up and running. And then the family come along and that's when the switch happened.

The Warrior (2002). (© FilmFour)

MW How did you manage to get *The Warrior* made?

AK I made a film called *The Sheep Thief*, which I shot when I was at the Royal College of Art – I didn't get into the National Film School. That was the film that really gave me the chance to make *The Warrior*.

No one in England was interested in a foreign-language film, but I met Bertrand [Faivre] at a festival in France, when I was traveling with my film and I pitched it to him and he was 'Great, let's do it', and we shook hands.

He didn't have an issue that the film wasn't in English. He gave us a little bit of money, for myself and my co-writer Tim Miller, to write. At the time I was directing commercials, even when I was at film school I would do the odd commercial to pay the bills. So I would write, then I'd go and scout for locations, then come back and write another draft.

So that film was made in a kind of idyllic way. I wasn't married, I didn't have kids, I didn't have a mortgage.

MW What was the budget in the end?

AK Two-and-a-half million. Film4 came on board. But that was normal, £2 million in those days was three people in a bed-sit wasn't it? That was what budgets were. We had an amazing experience on *The Warrior*. Being in India in the desert and in the Himalayas it was, 'This is why we want to make movies.' I don't think I've ever had as good an experience on a movie since.

MW What happened then? The next film you did was in America, wasn't it?

AK Yes. Because the one that I really wanted to do, I couldn't. I got sent a book that I loved – a western. And this is one of the challenges of our conversation right? Because the projects don't go away, I'm still dreaming I'm going to make this, it's not like it's dead, I'm just waiting for the right moment to pounce. There's always a kind of scary thing of mentioning the book that you love, which I'll mention to you, but I would just say that this is something that I still want to make.

Off the back of *The Warrior*, three of my heroes called up and said, 'We'd like to work with you.' Ridley Scott called up, Terrence Malick called up, and Scorsese called up.

So there were a lot of really exciting things. And then this book came along. I thought it was an amazing book, but it happened to be owned by Miramax. I started co-writing it and developing it – but to cut a long story short Harvey put the project into turnaround. He didn't get it. Because it was dealing with Native Americans.

So the film didn't happen but the script then went to Scorsese, then to Spielberg. He's still got it. That was a dream project that I really wanted to do, it was a really hot script, which I had my hands on, and I still can't believe it went.

MW Were there projects that you were developing yourself?

AK I was writing. It's hard to remember all those projects. I'm British, I'm a Londoner, I live here, I work here, but the ideas I've always been interested in are international. I think that's been a bit of the challenge. Funnily enough *Amy* became my London film. That's very much about North London, at a particular moment in time. Funnily enough, even on that one, we went to the BFI, thinking that finally we've got Amy Winehouse, it's set in London, it's Camden… And they passed on it. I have never had any money from them. I remember going to them after *Senna* and I said, 'I think this is going to be a really big hit. I would love to do something.' I wasn't allowed to meet the top person, I was meeting someone else, and the person I met, who I've known for many years, looked me in the eye and said, 'The issue is we're looking to work with first-time directors, which you're not, and world-class talent…'

MW There are so many first time directors who never make another film…

AK In France they have a fund to help you make a second movie. You have to somehow be a fighter in order to survive, to make the second, the third, the fourth, to have a career. You look at all the directors, I love, they've made a lot of movies. They made some bad ones, but the reason they had the chance to make the really good one is they were prolific. It's not easy here.

MW So you have a sort of freedom in documentary?

AK *Senna* was me working with Working Title and Universal Pictures, and sneaking through a documentary of which a large chunk isn't in English, and no-one's ever called it a foreign-language film. A film where the hero dies. And there was no development moment where you're like, 'Well, can he speak more English?' or 'Can he somehow miraculously survive?' And it was emotional, and it was a big hit, but

Senna (2010). (© Universal Studios/Working Title)

also it was a big learning curve. I didn't get paid well, it took years to make, I didn't get any back-end. I never shared the profits and it was a real fight, it was a real struggle. At that time I didn't have much money. That's why we set up our own company. So we owned more of *Amy*. You realise that if you're going to do all that work and it's not a huge budget, you need to own a chunk of the film.

MW   Was *Senna* Working Title's idea and they came to you?

AK   James had been developing it for a while and he had a first-look deal with Working Title. The honest truth is, they probably approached every director in town, before me. They all said no, for various reasons. Then eventually they did contact me. I'd never made a doc, but I love sport. And James knew that, because we met years ago, because I worked for a commercials company, when I was a student, which was owned by his stepdad, Mel Smith.

They were very clear. I was the hired director. It was 40 minutes of talking heads, 40 minutes of archive, 10 minutes of miscellaneous – that was how it was budgeted. I was essentially coming in to do the interviews.

I was told we were ready to go – green-lit. So I started, and for nine months, basically, the deal wasn't done. There was no deal. So, therefore, there was no budget. So I didn't get paid and I couldn't hire an editor. All I could do for nine months was look at the material, because I couldn't hire anyone. All I did was study it, and learn about the story and learn about the character. And then there's a moment when I thought: 'There is the film, I don't need to do interviews.'

I then basically spent the next few years saying to them, 'You don't need the interviews, but you still need me,' and they're thinking, 'Why do we need you? We just need a good editor.' And that was a proper row.

I did shoot some interviews, but I put the microphone in front of the person, and they were like, 'What the hell are you doing?' And I was like, 'I wanted to get good sound.' But basically I wouldn't shoot the interviews, because I knew that if I shoot them, they'll want to cut them in.

So we were looking at the footage, cutting the footage, thinking what the story is, looking for that footage. Everything was happening at the same time. I think that's what I found really exciting about the process. What I found restricting about fiction, was the classic process – write a script, cast it, raise the money, shoot it, edit it. I'd love to work on fiction in the way we work in documentary. To shoot and then go and edit then carry on shooting.

MW   And so how long was the whole process on *Senna*?

AK   Honestly, that film was nearly five years in the making. But editing was probably three years. My wife was like, 'What are you doing, spending all this time on a doc?' And I said, 'I think this could be really special and interesting and different.' And the first cut that I showed was over three hours just of archive. So every minute over 40, was 30 grand. So the film was way over budget, and they kept looking and going, 'He's nuts! These are YouTube clips!'

But they weren't paying, I got a fee and I was working for months, maybe even a year afterwards on no-fee.

The film was finished in 2010, it came out for some reason in Japan. I wasn't invited. It came out in Brazil, it didn't do well in Brazil. America dropped it – you know Focus had it and they dropped it. So the film was a failure. But then we took it to Sundance and it did really well and that's where it all started

MW   After *The Warrior* you shot *The Return* in America.

AK   That was just an awful experience of studio hell, and a lead actress who I felt didn't want to be there… it was madness. I think there's some interesting bits in there, I think some of it's really well directed but no one's ever seen it.

MW   The ones you were writing, were they set in India? Were they set in England? Do you remember any of them?

AK   Before I made *The Warrior*, I wrote a film set in Stoke Newington. My version of [Spike Lee's] *Do The Right Thing*. It was called *On The Corner*, our company now is basically named after that screenplay. That was meant to be the first film. I tried for quite a few years to get that made. British Screen put some money into it. But I couldn't crack the script.

It would have been a very different career path if I could have made *On The Corner*. It was lots of characters on the street, loads of incidents that happened while I was growing up, or things that happened to friends, funny things, violent things, petty crime, set in minicab offices and corner shops.

MW   So going to America was coincidence rather than a desire on your part, like, 'Let's get out?'

AK   I don't think I was trying to get out of the UK, but for everyone there's a point where you think, 'Okay it would be exciting.' And it is amazing working in the US, the crews are incredible, it looks so cinematic. That is a big thing for me. I love living here, but one of the reasons I love living here, is because it's kind of ordinary. And then I go to New York and I'm like, 'I want to shoot movies here.'

MW   Was *Far North* the same team as *The Warrior*?

AK   Pretty much. But with a UK crew. There were a lot of people who were whingers on that one. It was a really tough shoot because we were in the Arctic. I think the rudest crews I've worked with are the British. Because there's so much always going on here, you don't get the A-list, you don't get the B, you get the people who basically might do your job because there's nothing else, but they come in with whatever... their James Bond baseball cap and Harry Potter t-shirts, and this is like, so beneath them, doing your film. Whereas whenever I've worked abroad everyone's like, 'This is great'.

MW   That was the same producer?

AK   That was Bertrand.

AK   Because of the nature of where I wanted to shoot, the budget couldn't come down below a certain number. To get that budget we had to get cast, and to do the casting it made the language important, because the whole idea was that you can't do a film not in English, but then when you make a film in English and you want it to go to festivals they go, 'Well the fact that it's in English means it's kind of a compromise so we won't take it.' So it was a real learning curve, and this whole series of compromises worked against what initially I had wanted to do.

MW With *Amy* and with *Maradona*, were they your ideas? Or were they projects brought to you?

AK You know, I get offered a lot of projects and I say 'no' to all of them, and then occasionally something will come along and I'll say, 'I can do something with that'. *Amy* came off the back of *Senna*. James was at a dinner party with the head of Universal Music, who said, 'I really love *Senna*, would you be interested in doing Amy?' I thought, 'It's too soon to make a film about her'.

I said to James, 'We're not going to start, until they guarantee we have the music. Once we've got that in place I'll think about it. But if there's no music then there's no movie.' And so they went off and said, 'No, no, you'll get everything'.

Then I just started talking to people, because I was very aware that there was no go-to person, everyone was arguing, everyone hated each other, people were really damaged and building up trust was really the big thing.

I had a meeting with the head of the label, her dad, and the second manager, all of whom are in the film in some way, and I was saying to them, 'Look, I'll do this, but you have to just leave me alone. You can't interfere, you can't tell us what to do, you can't tell us who to talk to, just leave us alone for two years.' Then, fairly early on, I met her first manager [Nicky], who's in the film, who no one had really heard of at the time, and who really discovered her and who never made any money. And he and I connected. Without him I don't think I could have made the film.

So we got it all set up, we had the permissions, we had the music, we had the publishing of the music. I was never asked to write a treatment. On every other film up until then, at some point they'd go, 'Okay, now can you write that up', and then they'll be like,

Amy (2015). (© Universal Music Operations Limited)

'Well, can you change this', or 'What about that, what do you mean by this?' There'll be a person who sits at a desk, who develops. We didn't have any of that. That film, which started with a conversation, won an Oscar.

It is possible to make films without that development process. And I remember thinking at times, 'This is too heavy, this is too dark, this is not going to go down well with audiences. But it did really well and I remember thinking, 'Well this is the way I am going to work.'

MW   That development process is so rigid and formal, and you end up compromising just to get through it.

AK   I find it difficult when you have to go into a meeting and be told to sit in reception, and then you go in and you have to present your film to this person who's been there for 15 minutes. It's like, 'Who are you? What are these notes? How is that actually helping to get something made?' With documentaries I was able to dodge that. I was able to make stuff and there were none of those people in the middle. With fiction you're not allowed to say 'I don't know, but I'll figure that out.' You're meant to know everything and it doesn't always work for me.

And somehow, somewhere along the way, the joy is gone. Somewhere along the way, I'll be honest, I fell out of love with development. I fell out love with the idea that this is how a film has to be made.

MW   You did another fiction film after *Amy*, *Ali and Nino*. Did you develop the script?

AK   It was a book that I got sent, which I read and really liked, and then I worked with Christopher Hampton on it.

MW   And then you did a US TV series, *Mindhunter*.

AK   It was while I was making *Maradona*, I went off and did two episodes.

MW   Did someone bring you the idea of *Maradona*?

AK   You can see there is a recurring theme here, which is I obviously have no ideas. I'm a reactor. People say, 'What about this?', and I go, 'No. No. No. Maybe.' The guy who contacted me on that, contacted me after *Senna*, and I said, 'No. You just did a film about a Brazilian guy, do you want to do a film about an Argentinian?' But I am a big football fan. I always had a thing about Maradona being a really interesting character for a movie. No one else has ever lived a life like that. And so when that project came along, I thought about him for a while, but it didn't seem like the right time, and then it went away, and then it came back again. And then I thought, 'Well, actually this makes sense to do it as a third part of a trilogy of movies.' Netflix wanted it, as a series, they were chasing us, they were willing to offer a lot of money, but, for me, I wanted it to be something that people see on the big screen, around the world.

MW   Why do you think you can make more complex, darker documentary films compared to fiction? Do you think that's because of the audiences, or is it because of the financiers?

AK I think that's a really interesting question. It's all of the above, but primarily I think people in real life are so much more complex than anything that I could write. I remember every day on *Senna*, we'd go, 'If you wrote that, no one would believe you.' If the character, for example, of Jean-Marie Balestre, the guy who ran the sport, the French guy, if you wrote that character, the way he talks and wears those dark glasses, if you wrote those lines, you'd go, 'It's too much, tone it down.' If someone was acting that you'd say they were over-cooking it. I think Senna, Amy, Maradona, they're as big a star as these actors, but they're the real deal. He's really driving the car. The tension that comes from that is far greater than a person pretending on a green screen. Somewhere along the way I just stopped caring about someone pretending. It stopped having an emotional effect on me. I don't know what happened to me, but I got far more moved and affected by reality then I felt I would ever be by an actor pretending to be someone, or some actress who pretends to lose weight and has a bit of a hair and make-up job. I just... I don't know I want to see that, I want to see Amy – she's the best version of her.

Filmography

2001 *The Warrior*
2006 *The Return* (US film)
2007 *Far North*
2010 *Senna* (Documentary)
2015 *Amy* (Documentary)
2016 *Ali and Nino*
2017 *Mindhunter* (US TV series: 2 episodes)
2019 *Diego Maradona* (Documentary)
2021 *The Me You Can't See* (TV documentary mini series)

James Marsh

About a decade ago James directed *Red Riding 1980* for Revolution – one of three TV films based on the David Peace *Red Riding* novel trilogy. I was technically Executive Producer, but I was the sort of executive producer that I like as a director – the sort that is never there. So I had never really talked properly to James before. These are excerpts from a conversation that took place on 16 April 2020.

JM   How are things going at Revolution? Is it all ticking over okay?

MW   To be honest, one of the reasons I am doing this is to have a think about how to work. Revolution was set up to help us make the films we wanted to make – to give us that space. The idea wasn't to have a business, but just to avoid having someone tell us what to do.

JM   I think the whole landscape has changed so quickly, and I get the impression that what's going on now will accelerate changes that probably were looming anyway.

   I know that trying to put together a low-budget film is very difficult now.

MW   I feel like I've spent as long working on things that didn't get made as I have on the films themselves.

James Marsh on set, *Project Nim* (2011). (photo: David Dilley)

JM   That's the story of my life. I'm at a point in my life now where I look back and think I missed opportunities to make something that I really wanted to make. I am at an age where I can look back with regret. You kind of feel like your future is contracting, you may not have that many films left to make.

MW   Then you look at Ken Loach or Stephen Frears and you think, 'Okay, I've got a few years in the tank'.

JM   Yes. Hitchcock made *Psycho* when he was 59. Buñuel had a great late career. Robert Altman was a journeyman in television until his early forties. and suddenly had thirty, forty years of amazing productivity, did all his best work. I think perhaps, if I can flatter myself, I'm more that kind of filmmaker where I've had a career that's gradually built, and taken steps towards more ambitious things, but really slowly.

I was in New York in the Nineties and I was slowly making more and more ambitious documentaries and that ended up with me making a film called *Wisconsin Death Trip*. That was a film that was made with seed money from television, but actually it was an entirely independent film. One example of finding scraps of money and using your own money and gathering together a team of people who believe in what you are doing.

Beyond that, most of my work has probably emerged out of TV and the usual suspects of Film4 and BBC Film. That's been a model, I think, for many filmmakers of our generation. In a sense that is quite a benign system, compared to America – I lived in America for a while and it was much, much tougher to make a living there. It was almost impossible. I ended up leaving New York. When we left I had one nice sofa that my wife had bought from the Danish Consulate at a sort of fire sale they were doing, and that's all we had, and we had spent almost 15 years there.

MW   I thought *Wisconsin Death Trip* was made for *Arena* [a BBC documentary strand]?

JM   That's where it ended up. It's a long story. I was working on *Arena*, which was an amazing film school to go to. At that time TV was an exciting place because the lunatics were running the asylum, essentially. I worked for Anthony Wall and Nigel Finch and you could just do what you wanted. The pitching session was in a bar, you'd go to the bar and have a few drinks, and you'd say, 'This is what I want to do', and next thing you could be doing it. The first film I made for *Arena* was a film in Latin. I look back on that time now as an incredibly privileged, special time. You could make mistakes and there was no punishment. The more ambitious you were, the more likely you were to overreach, but you were encouraged to do that. There were no rules.

The last film I made for *Arena* whilst I was living in the UK was called *The Burger and the King*. Then, mainly for personal reasons, I moved to America in early '95. So then I was in America, trying to put together *Wisconsin Death Trip*, which took about four years. I had some seed money from *Arena*, and I got a little bit of money from a Norwegian immigrant fund in America.

And it took about three years to make that film. I did it in episodes. I'd shoot in one season. And then reflect on what I'd done and go and shoot some more the next season. Then run out of money. Then go back again. I had a team of people that began to believe in it. A very young DoP, Eigil Bryld. I met him because he had gone to school with my wife, in a small town in Denmark. She said he had shot a student film. And Eigil was 25 and he was about the only person who was mad enough to do it. Because we had no money and he was young, so didn't really need to make a living. We worked on it for three or four years with a producer, and eventually I showed it to people and no one really liked it. They hated it. But then the miracle was that it got into the Telluride Film Festival and then Venice. It had a festival life.

But that didn't really lead to very much. I'm guessing based on your productivity that you always have something to go on to straight away. For me, that limbo between projects always made me very depressed. You want to make something, you have ideas, but you can't get them made.

MW Did you work with the same people on *The King*?

JM Yes, I used the same producer, and again that was a slow-burn project. Ben Ross was an old friend of mine from University and his sister –

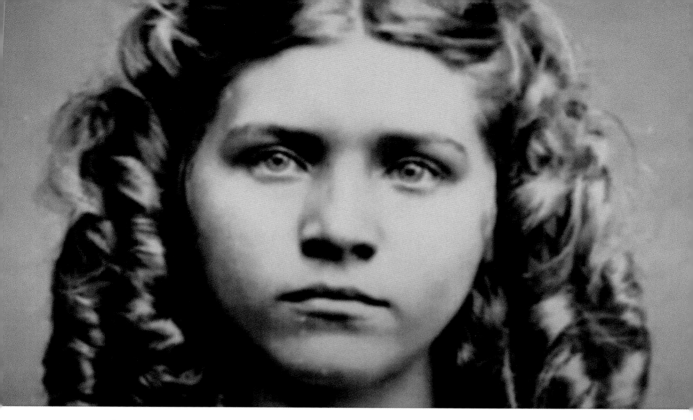

Wisconsin Death Trip (1999). (© BBC/Hands On Productions)

Tessa – was running Film4. I was desperate for money. I had no money at all. I was living in New York and we moved out of a rent-controlled apartment, because we couldn't afford it, to an even cheaper apartment in Brooklyn. So Ben very kindly told his sister I was in trouble, and she gave me some development money to generate a project for Film4. It wasn't exactly nepotism because I had made *Death Trip*. So I got this small amount of money from Film4, and then slowly built the script with a writer who was also down on his luck, called Milo Addica.

That was a very difficult writing process. When we started he was basically living in his car out in LA, but during the time we were writing, Milo's film *Monster's Ball* got made and was incredibly successful and he got an Academy Award nomination.

I managed to attach Gael García Bernal and so that film got made, but it got made in the worst possible way.

MW   So you were making films set in America because you were living there?

JM   I'd made quite a few documentaries that were based in America. I guess this is a slightly different conversation than you would have with a filmmaker who was based in Britain throughout their career. I was trying to have it both ways and ended up having it neither way. I wasn't getting much traction in America, and I felt slightly divorced from the UK.

MW   Do you feel you the same space exists in the fiction films as you had in the documentaries?

JM   I don't think it does at all. Firstly, I don't write most of the dramas I have done. I've tormented screenwriters, but I've not written a lot myself. In documentaries you really feel like you are the author. I often shot a lot of the films myself. I always do the first cut. So the sense of authorship is just vastly more. I guess your investment is therefore deeper, by virtue of that.

MW   What would you say were the factors that made you want to move away from documentary?

JM   I'd always had the ambition to be a proper, dramatic filmmaker. I didn't go to film school – film schools weren't really around when I was a student. So I just took what I thought was the path of least resistance to making movies. So *Wisconsin Death Trip* was for me a conscious choice to make a dramatised documentary that had no real conventional documentary elements in it, but was still a documentary because it used original source materials. Dramatic filmmaking was always my ambition. Documentaries was something that I was doing to make a living, because in Britain it was easy to make a documentary.

Then looking back you realise how lucky you were.

What happened after *The King* was that I became utterly unemployable. It went to Cannes and that for me was going to be the great moment, you've got the red carpet and Cannes is the high-water mark of auteur cinema, and the première goes very well, and it gets a standing ovation, as most films do, and the next morning I go to do the press, and then I see the publicist sort of shuffling the *Hollywood Reporter* and the *Variety* so I can't see them. I saw the face and thought, 'Okay, I know that something's gone wrong here'. But I can't stop myself reading *Variety*, and it is the most horrible review you could ever read about a film that you've made. It's just awful. And there's a *Rolling Stone* review that comes in a bit later that likens it to being stabbed in the stomach for two hours. And they keep coming, these reviews. They're all bad.

So the best morning of my life then becomes the worst morning of my life. Now I've turned from being the auteur on his way to being a Cannes favourite to this sort of fucking loser, whose film is reviled by almost everybody.

That film stopped my career dead, I couldn't do anything. I'd been away from documentaries for six years and that landscape had changed in my absence. I had lost my contacts at the BBC. So I was unemployed for two and a half years – and I had two young children at this time living in the apartment in Brooklyn. It was a really miserable time. I remember looking at adverts for Starbucks thinking, 'At a certain point I'm going to have to go and do this, because I've got no money.'

The one thing I could get going was a film about Diane Arbus, the photographer. But then, bizarrely, I got offered a terrible horror movie for some crappy little LA outfit. So I gave up the Diane Arbus film and pissed off her daughter, who was going to give me the rights to make the film. It was a horrible period.

Then Simon Chinn, the producer of *Man on Wire,* called me up and said, 'I've got this idea about this guy who walked between the twin towers.' I knew the story because I had been to the twin towers once with an ex-girlfriend of mine, whose brother worked at a firm called Cantor Fitzgerald, and he told me the story and I thought, 'Oh, that's fucking amazing'.

So when Simon called me I thought, 'Fuck, this is the best idea ever'. It is a beautiful story.

Then I had to go through the process of befriending Philippe Petit, which was one of the hardest things I've done in my life, because he's a very difficult man.

MW That's the problem with documentaries, isn't it?

JM Exactly, every single one has one figure like that, who you have to do this prolonged and very careful dance with. If you step on their toes once – it's all over.

He jealously guarded his story and he didn't like me initially. He didn't like anybody very much, to be honest.

So I threw myself into that. I'd run out of money, so I had to move my wife and children back to Denmark. I had to sleep on my friend's floor – who was a professor at Columbia – and write the outline for *Man on Wire.*

The more I found out about the story, the more I thought, 'This is just brilliant'. The spying on the twin towers, the whole caper movie feel, which he was very consciously living out. I felt I could bring some of the things I learned from making features – how to tell a story in a dramatic, narrative way. It was a good hybrid. It's the only film I've made that I actually like.

Then when Phillipe Petit saw it, he absolutely hated the film, he disowned it and wrote me this 17-page, handwritten letter, basically to say what a terrible human being I am, listing all the things I got

Man on Wire (2008). (© Wall to Wall (Egypt) Ltd/UK Film Council)

wrong. His main problem was with the windows in the reconstructions – they were wrong. He was obsessed with this. I had to point out that, 'Well, Philippe, the building isn't there, I couldn't shoot in the real building because it's gone.' I'd done an amazing job to get that building for free. I got in there for a weekend having blagged my way in by being nice to people.

Then I made *Red Riding* [for Revolution]. I knew Tony Grisoni [the writer] a bit, and he slipped me a script before you knew. Then Andrew [Eaton] got in touch with me.

And by the way, Michael, that was probably my happiest experience making a drama. It was a very special project, I think, for many people involved. I'd made *The King* and I hadn't worked well with actors, I had no idea how to talk to them, and by the time I'd figured that out, the film was over and I'd already messed up. Then coming to *Red Riding* and working with British actors, I think they actually want to help you. They're actually nice. They'll talk to you. They will rehearse with you. They'll put the costume on, and they'll do the lines for you, without arguing. They'll go through the door that you want them to go through. William Hurt wouldn't go through a door if he didn't want to go through that door. If he didn't want to go through that door: 'I'm not going through that door. That door handle's wrong. I'm not going through that door.' But, you know, Warren Clarke wasn't like that.

But then I made some bigger feature films, I went to Working Title and took a step into a sort of studio world…

MW You see those as studio films rather than independent?

JM Definitely. No question, they are studio films. The first experience with Working Title was good. The script came to me from the screen-writer, who liked *Man on Wire*, and thought that there was an emotional register in that film that he saw in Stephen Hawking's life story. So he suggested me to Working Title who grudgingly said, 'Okay, well maybe he's the right man to do this.'

That was a very good experience.

MW Is it your relationship to the other people that makes it feel like a studio film?

JM You have less authorship for sure. The casting was my choice, but it still has to be agreed. There's a whole process. Focus [groups] were very hostile to the film and they wanted to do re-shoots, but it tested very well in London.

And to Eric Fellner's great credit, he said, 'We'll test it in America and if it tests well there, this is the version we want to show.'

MW How long before the shoot did you come on? Were you working with the writer for a while?

JM Yeah, I came on about nine months before we shot the film, and worked with the writer and the producer, Lisa Bruce. Anthony McCarten, the writer, who was more of a novelist at this point, had been working on it for ten years, and trying to get permissions from Jane Hawking to use her memoir. So this was a little cottage industry project at this point.

MW On *The Mercy* and *King of Thieves*, were you involved in developing those projects? How much are they your projects?

JM *The Mercy* was Studio Canal. It was basically a studio film. Colin Firth was already attached to do it. The big mistake of that project was trying to make a big-budget film out of a story of someone going mad and killing themselves. He is a loser and a deceiver and that sort of story doesn't really support a big budget.

MW Was *Shadow Dancer* something you developed?

JM It was in the aftermath of *Man on Wire*. I got sent quite a bit of stuff at that time. It was written by Tom Bradby, who's the ITN newsreader now, but then he was a correspondent.

It was this simple idea of espionage within a domestic situation. The idea of spying on your own family. What would that be like? The intimacy of the betrayal. So I rewrote the script with Tom. I cast Andrea Riseborough and then Clive Owen committed to it. Without Clive the film wouldn't have got made. It's as simple as that. And that was a really nice collaboration, Clive's a really good actor to work with, he's very generous, he's one of us. It was a low-budget film. He has no airs and graces.

I think BBC Film were involved in that one. *Project Nim* was BBC Film as well.

MW I didn't realise that. So did *Project Nim* get a theatrical release in the UK?

JM   Yes. They had high hopes for it, but I knew they were misguided because it basically was a very sad story.

MW   It's a great film, by the way. But not everyone comes out of it well... was that difficult? I was wondering to what extent, did you feel awkward at all? I mean, if they'd seen the film and gone, 'Well, I don't like the way I'm coming out of it' were they in a position where they could stop it?

JM   At Sundance, for the first screening, I had all the people apart from the professor, sitting behind me during the first screening of the film. They hadn't seen it yet, and that was quite a difficult experience but...

MW   The professor is the person who comes out of it worst.

JM   There was more than I was able to put in the film, because of the way he treated women and so on, but the film was Nim's story, it was a biography of a chimpanzee, essentially. But the professor got very angry about the film. He couldn't come to Sundance because the women wouldn't have him there. They said, 'If he comes we're not coming.'

      My future, Michael, might well be back in documentaries, because I'm thinking that they're viable in a way that features are not now.

MW   You're the author of your documentaries.

JM   After the *King of Thieves*, and *The Mercy*, and *Theory of Everything* – which was a studio film too – I kind of yearn to only have to answer to myself again. So even before this happened with Covid, I thought, 'I need to go make a documentary again, I need to get honest again, to get back to more control, more authorship.' I wasn't living those last two in the way I want to live a film, where it just takes you over, and everything you do and everything you feel is about the film.

MW   Is that something you feel is absent as a possibility in fictional film, especially in Britain?

JM   I think it can exist. I would say that for *Red Riding* it existed, which was an unusual project in many ways. *Shadow Dancer*, for sure, was an independent film where it was my cut. But the studio films, the three I've done, essentially one after the other, have put me in a situation where I don't feel I want to do another one of those, maybe ever again.

So, I've got two or three ideas I'm working on now, that are documentaries. I think documentaries, like at the start of my career, might be the path of least resistance to make a film.

MW Are there things that you've tried to get made, that haven't got made?

JM I've been trying to make this film based on a dream diary. I was doing some research into dreams and dream theory, and I came upon an archive of a sleep research centre, in the University of California at Santa Cruz, and they've archived dream diaries, some of which are hundreds of years old. People have written down their dreams. They gave me a diary of a man in Toronto, who'd written down only dreams about the woman he was in love with all his life. So his dream diary is a love story. His life story runs parallel to this, because he ends up marrying this woman and the dreams reflect that. And he has an affair at a certain point and the dreams reflect that. Then his wife gets ill, with cancer, and she dies. And his dreams reflect all that.

I wrote a script based on these dreams, and organised them as a progression. The whole story is told through these dreams.

And I tell people and they look like, 'What the fuck are you talking about?'

So it's one that I feel will only ever exist in my head.

MW I feel with documentary, at quite an early stage of the development you get the money and you know you're making the film. Whereas, with fiction there is often such a long process of formal development. For me it is easier and quicker and more enjoyable and better if you're able to start from a vaguer place, to begin making the film, before you know exactly what it is going to be. A long, drawn-out development process feels very mechanical.

JM   I think that what you don't make defines you as much as what you do make. We've all had other careers we could have had.

MW   Better careers.

JM   I've made huge mistakes, but I still have some work that means something, I think, to me and to other people. So I have regrets, and I have things I wish I'd done. I wish I had another 40 years to make films. I wish I'd made more films, because I think I'd be a better filmmaker if I'd made more.

Filmography

1999   *Wisconsin Death Trip* (US docudrama)
2005   *The King* (US)
2005   *The Team* (US documentary)
2008   *Man on Wire* (Documentary)
2009   *Red Riding: The Year of Our Lord 1980* (TV Movie)
2011   *Project Nim* (Documentary)
2012   *Shadow Dancer*
2014   *The Theory of Everything*
2016   *The Night Of* (US TV Mini-Series: 1 episode)
2017   *The Mercy*
2018   *King of Thieves*

Andrew Haigh

These are excerpts from a conversation that took place on 1 May 2020. Andrew was in Los Angeles.

MW   You had a lot of success with *Weekend* and *45 Years* but you then made your next film in America. Do you live in America?

AH   I live here part-time to be close to family, but I also like making films in the US. In a way, I never really felt part of the UK film industry, even though I've made two films there. I don't know other directors. I don't know a lot of producers. I don't feel part of the scene there. Working in America also seems to offer a larger canvas to tell your stories.

MW   You just feel it's more cinematic, America? It seems to me that there are certain stories that are quite small that you can tell in America, and they can be watched all over the world. Whereas if you tell a small story in England, it's kind of, 'Oh, it's very specific to Nottingham'. or 'It's very specific to Norfolk', or whatever. People are more willing to watch films from America than the UK.

AH   I think that's true. The scope of your stories can certainly be bigger, along with the possible audience. But art-house cinema is still a tough

Andrew Haigh, on set, *45 Years* (2015) (photo: Agatha A. Nitecka)

sell whether you are making it in the US or the UK. It's perhaps even harder in America. It's difficult to even talk about making a 'drama' unless you can find some element of genre within it or a famous actor to sell it.

MW How did you get started in film?

AH I got a job after university at Merchant Ivory working for Ismail Merchant and Paul Bradley. They were forever wheeling and dealing to get their films made. They were a successful company, and still it was a struggle to get any project off the ground. What was interesting was how many projects were almost made, so many films in the development cabinet that never quite got financed.

MW At the time of *Greek Pete* you were working as an assistant film editor?

AH I was assistant editor on and off for ten years after working in production. I always wanted to direct, but editing meant I could pay the bills and work in the industry. I had struggled to make anything myself for a long time, but I was really influenced by the micro-budget features coming out of the US by the likes of Joe Swanberg. They were making features on their own for nothing. I made *Greek Pete* in 2008. It cost under 6k and got released in one cinema in London, which at the time felt like a real success. In the same year, I made a short film under the 'Cinema Extreme' banner for Film4. Both of those projects did okay for what they were, but then I went back to being an assistant while I tried to get *Weekend* off the ground. To put it mildly, no-one was very interested in making that film.

MW Who gave you the money in the end?

AH There was one exec, Anna Seifert-Speck, who worked at EM Media, out of Nottingham, and she was the only one who really supported it. She was determined to make it. She essentially kickstarted my whole career. I think we shot *Weekend* for 60k with another 40k for post-production.

I wish the funding bodies would do that more. I wish they would give filmmakers a small amount of money and say, 'Do you know what, just fucking go and do something. We're not even going to give you any notes, just and go do something, see what you can do, and then come back to us when you're done.'

MW   Was one of the reasons for going to America – the budget?

AH   Not really. *45 Years* came after *Weekend*, and I think the budget was around 2.5 million for that, which felt like a lot of money at the time. We could shoot on film and had a generous schedule. We always wanted *Lean on Pete* to come after *45 Years*, so it was less the money that drew us to the US and more the project.

MW   With *Lean on Pete*, that was your idea? Did you raise the money within your production company?

AH   I fell in love with the book, and my producer Tristan, UK-based, raised the money. Most of the money was out of the UK through the BFI and Film4, with A24 in the US putting money in as a pre-sale. The total budget was around 7 million dollars.

MW   The story is not an obviously commercial story. Do you think you would have got the same budget, from the same financiers, if it had been set in Yorkshire rather than America?

AH   No. They wouldn't have done it. I think they would be terrified that it would become a very small film about English poverty and class. I mean the truth is that not many people saw *Lean on Pete* anyway. The issue became that because I was now making it in America, suddenly there was a desire, both from the US side and from the UK side, to make it more commercial. Throughout the process, I would say, 'I don't think this is a commercial film, it's not what you think it is.' It's not a sweet story about a kid and a horse. It doesn't have that uplifting ending those films need. If I'm honest, it felt like a battle

45 Years (2015). (© The Bureau/Film4/BFI/Creative England/UK Film Council/
The Match Factory)

making that film, especially when it came to marketing it. I could see there was a desire to sell the movie in a way that wasn't what the film was. But it cost nearly 7 million dollars, and nobody wants to lose their investment.

I often feel like as a career goes on, it gets progressively harder, rather than easier, to make the films you really want to, especially if those films don't play in the commercial arena.

MW I think that's an interesting point. I guess that is what pushes people to either go to do bigger, studio films, or TV.

Lean on Pete (2017). (© The Bureau/Film4/BFI)

AH Yes. We all want to work. I did an HBO show called *Looking* after *Weekend*. I directed the pilot, and then I stayed on to be the showrunner for two seasons. I'd just done *Weekend* which cost under 100k and the HBO half-hour is something like $2 million per episode, and I was like: 'What the fuck? Okay, I'm going to do this.' I'd never directed on a set with more than 15 people. It taught me a huge amount and was a pretty special experience. It also meant I got paid for once, which is nice if you work in low-budget films.

But at the same time, the television work has to feel like an extension of the film work. I have to care about it to the same degree. At the moment, I'm finishing another TV project called *The North*

Water for BBC2. I saw it more as a five-hour film, and that is also the attraction of TV. It allows you to expand your storytelling.

MW Was that with the same producer that you worked with on the films?

AH No, it was with See-Saw. They came to me with the book five years ago. TV takes so long, doesn't it?

MW TV's even worse than film.

AH Absolutely, forever. I wrote the pilot before I shot *Lean on Pete.* So it takes a long, long time. But everything does.

MW Why do you think it takes so long?

AH There's so much pressure on every project to be successful. So you end up in a long, drawn-out development process with different voices, all in a state of anxiety over whether it's working. The frustrating thing is that then the shoot and the post-production is often so constricted by tight television schedules that you don't always feel you have the time to bring the magic to the material.

MW I've been talking to quite a few people whose first films were low budget, so they had a lot of freedom. Then, as they tried to move on, that freedom got less. They had to shift a little to try and keep someone happy, they have to try and cast it to make it more commercial, or...

AH I feel that's exactly what happens. You may not feel it at the time, but there's immense freedom making your first low-budget film. You are discovering your voice. People let you be. And then it gets complicated. You have to build on your previous work. Suddenly there are expectations, and this only gets worse the bigger the budgets become. I feel more anxious with each new film, not less. Do I risk doing something different, or should I stick with what I know? Making *Weekend,* I got very few notes, but I get more notes with each project. And you listen to those notes.

MW I think often you compromise, not in a cynical way, but because you are persuaded. You are genuinely trying to find a way of making the film

AH Absolutely. You want the project to be made, and you have your own insecurities too. If someone has an issue with a scene, you begin to question it. Sometimes they are right, and the notes help you push deeper into the material. And then sometimes they are wrong. The trick is to work out when they are right or when they are wrong. There is nothing worse than being in the edit knowing you made a change to please someone that was never going to work. You have to be able to stand by your choices. You have to keep your individual voice even if it's not to everyone's taste all of the time.

MW It feels like in the UK if you go above a certain budget level, which is low, then there is a pressure on the film to be commercial

AH I feel like the minute you get over about 3 million then there is a signifiant pressure for it to be more commercial, more attractive to the US market. And you know what, maybe that is fair enough. 3 million is a lot of money, but it limits the kind of projects we make in the UK.

MW Do you think there's a whole bunch of types of films that you want to make that you self-censor in a way. That you feel 'Oh that's not going to happen.' You find yourself looking for a sweet spot between what you want to do and what's possible,'?

AH I do feel like that. I've got a few projects that I deeply love, perhaps the ones I am most passionate about, but can't get them made. They are a little too expensive and not commercial enough. It is not as if I have the right to make anything I want with someone else's money, but it's depressing to think they may never see the light of day. In the meantime, you adapt, and you search for something that can be made while still speak to why you became a filmmaker in the first place.

Filmography

2009 *Greek Pete*
2011 *Weekend*
2015 *45 Years*
2014 *Looking* (US TV series)
2016 *Looking* (US TV movie)
2017 *Lean on Pete* (US film)
2019 *The OA* (US TV series: 2 episodes)
2021 *The North Water* (4-part TV mini series, completed but not yet released)

Carol Morley

These are excerpts from a conversation that took place on 28 April 2020.

CM I just want to say before we start that I really wanted to make feature films and it wasn't happening, and I was reading an article about you in which you said, 'There's too many British filmmakers sitting on their arses in development. You just have to go and do it.' And I feel like that actually catapulted me into a different headspace, because I think that while there are so many factors that limit the amount of films you make, or prevent someone making a film in the first place – it could be money, it could be that you doubt your ideas, or yourself, it could be many things – I think ultimately it's a release from all of that to acknowledge that maybe you don't need so much money or maybe you don't need the best idea in the world, or maybe the idea will develop, or maybe you're not looking at your idea in the right way. So I think there's all these elements, which contribute to why you don't do something. For me as a filmmaker it's that battle between owning your own demons and the demons that the world puts in your way. Even if it's a low-budget film, it's still a lot of money. And even if you begin making a very low-budget film – as I did with *The Alcohol Years*

Carol Morley (right), on set, *Out of Blue* (2018). (photo: Skip Bolen)

– you have aspirations to do more than that and eventually what you want to do will probably require more money.

When I was about 23 I was living in London doing lots of different jobs, like working in shops. I was desperate to do something so I did A-Levels at night school in Film Studies and Photography. Then I went to Central Saint Martins to study Fine Art and Film, and what I learned there, which has maybe slowed me down in my filmmaking, is that it's not just the story that you're telling that is important, it's how you tell it.

So I think part of my personal slowness is that I'm really quite obsessed with HOW you tell the story. So you end up writing your own work and it definitely takes time to incubate and to develop.

The Alcohol Years came out of making a number of Arts Council funded films, fine art films which no one saw as fine art enough. I didn't really fit into that world.

The Alcohol Years was meant to be a ten-minute thing for the Arts Council. The budget wasn't a lot – £50,000 or less.

MW All from the Arts Council?

CM No! The Arts Council gave, I can't remember, maybe £8,000. And then we had to go to all these other places for the rest of the money. At first it got turned down by Channel 4. That's the history of my career. I always get turned down. That's the thing that you learn, don't accept being turned down. Go back. I would wait for the person who turned it down to leave and then re-apply. Which is another reason it takes a long time. You have to wait for that person in power to leave!

With *The Alcohol Years* we (Cairo Cannon, my long-term producer, and I) went to another commissioner at Channel 4 – who did late-night stuff. I think he had ten grand to give to each project. He took the idea to a meeting but they turned it down because though they were looking for more personal projects, it didn't fit with their brief. But then he went, 'But fuck it, I'm giving you the money anyway.' People like that, who are prepared to take a risk, make a huge difference to a film coming into existence.

I was at Saint Martins from 1990 to 1993 and I started to make *The Alcohol Years* in '98. It came out in 2000. You have to keep your hold of what you want to be and why you want to do it. And that is what gets eroded, I think. That's what gets eroded as a filmmaker, because there are so many elements that you can encounter.

MW That area between having the idea and getting it made is such a difficult area and often so long. It is where a producer really helps. You've had the same producer on all of your films?

CM Yes, Cairo Cannon. We met at an evening class in East London – she's from America originally, and she was in the theatre but we met at this evening class in experimental film at Four Corners [film and photography centre]. I'd got my first Arts Council grant and I said, 'Would you produce it?' She hadn't produced anything before, but she had all the immediate qualities I felt a producer needs; a lot of tenacity, a lot of energy. So we set off learning together, really. We've also worked with other producers and learned from them along the way, because everybody's got different experiences that are really helpful. And film is so collaborative.

MW I loved your book *7 Miles Out* – which covers some of the same territory as *The Alcohol Years*.

CM What happened there was I was trying to make *Dreams of a Life*, but it wasn't happening. That was heart-breaking, because nobody wanted it. That got turned down by the BFI three times, and Film4 three times.

So from the frustration of that I wrote *7 Miles Out* because I was talking to my niece who was a teenager, and I said, 'Oh, my film's not happening,' and she said, 'If you write a book, it exists. In that form. Even if it isn't published. If you've got a script and you don't make it – the film doesn't exist.' So that drove me to write *7 Miles Out* because I thought I might actually go mad. I had to do something that, even if it would never get published, would be complete in itself. It came out of that period of frustration.

After *The Alcohol Years* there was a story I'd read when I was 13, called 'Food Farm', in this women's science-fiction anthology [*Fat*, ed. Kit Reed, 1974]. I got in touch with the writer of it [Kit Reed], and we got the rights for it. But we were working with another production company and they said, 'You don't write, we need to hire a writer.' So it got taken away and the screenplay didn't work as people wanted it. So that died. Now I would go, 'I'm writing it and it will get made, fuck it.'

There was something I wrote called *The Trials of Liz and Alex*. It was a road trip of two young women, tracing the British witch trials. But that didn't happen. I wish I'd gone, 'Let's just make it'. But there is always that element that you do need some money.

And then there was a documentary about Joy Division in China. I went to China with the producer Natasha Dack and we found a girl group that covered Joy Division songs. My idea was to bring them back to Manchester and see Manchester and Joy Division through the eyes of these young women. But that didn't happen.

Peter Carlton was interested in financing it at Film4 but then no one else was, so it just died.

MW   It always strikes me that when you make a film you've got no idea whether it's going to work or not, especially if there's a documentary element or an improvised element to it. It's quite random which are the ones that get made and which are the ones that don't, and which are the ones that turn out well and which are the ones that don't.

Dreams of a Life (2011). (Courtesy Ronald Grant/Mary Evans)

CM   I really believe there's an audience for everything, and if you are fascinated with the story, probably someone else would be. With *Dreams of a Life* it was private money that kick started the film. It came from Danielle Ryan – she was part of Ryanair. She put the first money in so that I could do a couple of interviews… I did Martin, who's the key part of *Dreams of a Life*. And Martin's interview was extraordinary. But people still didn't want to make the film.

MW   *Dreams of a Life* came out in 2011. Were you able to live off the money you were getting from your work in film between *The Alcohol Years* and *Dreams of a Life*?

CM   No! At that point I was teaching film and video at an American university based over here. At one point I applied for a job in America at the California Institute of the Arts, because I was so fucked off, I thought, 'I can't take anymore, I can't take this country, I can't take…' you know, 'I'm just not making things, I'm not making what I want to make.' So I went for this job interview, and I stayed with a friend and he went, 'What do you want at the end of your life? Do you want to be this teacher, or do you want to be a filmmaker?' And I went, 'I want to be a filmmaker,' and he went, 'Go and fucking do it then.'

MW   I imagine *Dreams of a Life* was an incredibly hard film to pitch.

CM   I felt that people were interested in the story, but they didn't understand the way I wanted to tell it, which was not totally factual or conclusive. I think the feeling for the film I wanted to make came from when I was on the tube and picked up *The Sun* newspaper, where on page 7 there was the headline 'skeleton of Joyce found on sofa with the telly still on', and as soon as I saw it I said to myself, 'I'm going to make a film about Joyce Vincent, even if I never find out anything about her. And I'm going to make it a musical!' I mean I just knew at this point that I wanted to bring something beyond grimness to the story. Some light. Then when I met Joyce Vincent's boyfriend Martin he said, 'Joyce always wanted to be a singer', and I'm like, 'Oh fuck it, I knew'. I did a lot of research into her life and found a lot of people who knew her, but the way I wanted to make the film was always to include the conflicting stories about Joyce, and to emphasise the gaps, and to create scenes with Joyce Vincent played by an actress – Zawe Ashton – that were imagined parts of her life. I wanted a very open film. In a way it was a mystery that was never solved and that never gave easy answers.

MW   How long was that process between reading the article and getting the money to get started on the film?

CM   Probably three years. Nobody was interested in it. I typed a letter to the BFI complaining, a very formal letter. But they turned it down again, so I handwrote another letter and I wrote in lipstick: 'Fund my film'. I heard they thought it was blood and it was pinned on the wall of the head of film at the time.

And then Katherine Butler took over at Film4. I remember meetings with her that were hours long, hours. But eventually Film4 came on board. And then the BFI came on board. But the first people on board were the Irish Film Board, who said it could fit their remit because the film was about death, and death was an Irish preoccupation!

The difference between making something and not is pure tenacity.

MW   Which is exhausting

CM   The weird thing is you spend all these years on a film and then you get so few fucking days to actually shoot it. You're like, 'What was that all about? Wow!' But it is all part of filmmaking – the pain, the waiting, the frustration – all of that is being a filmmaker.

So in the end with *Dreams of a Life* the first public money was from the Irish Film Board. So we had to film a lot of it in Ireland. I had to do all my post-production in Ireland.

MW   So you got the London Film Board for your Manchester film, and the Irish Film Board for your London film?

CM   Yeah.

MW   And what was the budget?

CM   £500,000.

MW   And did that then transform the kind of way you could then go about preparing your next film? Were people then asking you what you wanted to do?

CM   Only as in 'What is the next documentary you would like to make?' But I don't consider myself a documentary filmmaker, more a filmmaker that works in different ways. And that then is a stumbling block. I got development money from BFI, but when I delivered the first draft the BFI was really surprised because they thought it was going to be a documentary, but I'd written a screenplay.

I think women often end up a lot in the documentary world because it's cheaper to make. And a cursory look at budgets will show that women get smaller budgets.

MW There's a lot of small budgets knocking around. The problem is how to live on the money from small budgets. You did a film called *Edge*?

CM Yeah. We were trying to make *Dreams of a Life* and I read what you said about getting off your arse and that's when we made *Edge*. And we made *Edge* for fifty grand. That was private money. It was something I'd written and we improvised with actors. We made it with no money, virtually no money and that did give us a lot of energy I think.

MW Was that a feature length film?

CM That was feature length, yeah. And you know, it's not perfect, but it was for me a really great experience of working with great actors and feeling that energy of a fiction film

MW So with *The Falling* did you then have to persuade people that you could do a much more dramatic film? Or did the script sell itself?

CM I feel sometimes that a screenplay is a really important craft but it is not the film… any screenplay that you read post-film is not what they shot, you know. It's not the one that was on set. It is edited to match the film. So I will probably put more dialogue in a script than I want, because you can cut that easily, but at least you have it. But often when somebody from the world of script readers reads the script, they expect to see the film on the page. Whereas for me it's the possibility of the film that is on the page, it's the possibility of getting everything shot that you need. But in development the screenplay becomes this template that everyone's poring over and while that's important, so much does change when you start to shoot it.

MW   Is *The Falling* an adaptation or is it your own original screenplay?

CM   It was inspired by a lot of medical articles I read.

MW   You had a lot of success with that film. Then your next film was in America. A lot of British filmmakers go to America. Is there some aspect of making a film in America that seems more attractive than making a film in Manchester?

CM   Well, I think that we all grew up watching American films, you know. They seemed like real films! But for me what brought me to America with that film was that Luc Roeg, who had produced *The Falling* with Cairo Cannon, went, 'Oh, my dad [Nic Roeg] always wanted to do this book by Martin Amis and he never managed to do it. And I went, 'I want to do it.' That was even before I'd read it.

    Then I read the book – it's called *Night Train* – and I thought, 'I really feel like I could rescue the characters from the pages of this book, especially the women of this book.' I think I have a thing in all my films of rescuing women from their situations. [The film is called *Out of Blue*.]

MW   And that was BBC Film?

CM   And the BFI.

MW   It just happened to be set on location in America?

CM   Yeah. I very much saw it as America through a British lens.

MW   What are you working on now?

CM   I just delivered a second draft of a script the other week – to BFI and BBC Film. I got a Wellcome Screenwriting Fellowship a few years ago – they give you thirty grand for the year to do anything to do with science and health – a long and in-depth research period – which was amazing. And they had this archive of 80 boxes of somebody called Audrey Amiss who was born in Sunderland in 1933, came to London in the Fifties, studied painting at the Royal Academy of Arts, and in

Out of Blue (2018). (© Cannon and Morley Productions/Independent/Ellenglaze Films/
The Electric Shadow Company/BBC Film/Dignity Film Finance/British Film Institute/
Particular Crowd/Gorean Films)

her final year didn't complete, because she had this massive psychotic breakdown. And she ended up as this revolving-door psychiatric patient. She lived in Clapham for 50 years, 30 years with her mum, and she was a typist for the Civil Service until she retired. But, she kept her art going. She was very funny. So when her nephew and niece went in her flat after she died aged 79 in 2013, they found 50,000 sketches, all her diaries, and all her letters, which I've read. She's absolutely brilliant. So I've written a film – a road movie through her life called *Typist Artist Pirate King!*, which is how she referred to herself in her passport when you used to have to put your occupation.

Filmography

2000   *The Alcohol Years* (Documentary)
2010   *Edge*
2011   *Dreams of a Life* (Documentary)
2014   *The Falling*
2018   *Out of Blue* (US film)

Edgar Wright

These are excerpts from a conversation that took place on 5 May 2020. Edgar was working on a new film, set in London, called *Last Night in Soho*.

EW We were about to do a five-days reshoot and then do another preview quickly, and then lock it up, because it was supposed to come out in September. Now it looks like it's going to come out in April next year.

MW You were unusually young when you made your first feature?

EW I was at Bournemouth Art College for two years, not on the film course, I couldn't get onto the film course, they wouldn't let me in. At the end of the course I made a movie, a very silly, spoof movie – and off the back of it, I got an agent in London and through it I met a lot of comedians like David Walliams and Matt Lucas and then, later, Simon Pegg. I made the film in the summer of '94, for £11,000. The money came from the local newspaper editor, who wanted to invest in the movie and I came to London to edit it [the film was *A Fistful of Fingers*]. I was signing on, and sleeping on my brother's floor, and editing the movie, and around that time I started going to see some stand-up shows, and my friend took me to a show where Matt Lucas

Edgar Wright on the set of *Shaun of the Dead* (2004). (© Rogue Pictures/courtesy Everett Collection/Mary Evans)

was performing. And I went straight up to him after and said, 'Hey, that was amazing. I've made a movie and I'm going to make another movie, would you be in it?' So I became friends with him.

Matt and David went for a meeting at the Paramount comedy channel, and they were doing a show called *Mash and Peas*, and they said, 'Oh, our friend Edgar is a film director, he's got a film on release right now, it's at the Prince Charles.'

It was at the Prince Charles for two weeks. So that's how I got my first TV job.

So, then I started doing TV when I was very young – about 22. It was amazing that I was there at all, I have to pinch myself, that I was actually directing comedy shows when I was 22... 23. I think some of the crew used to hate it, that I was just a kid from Somerset, who hadn't even been to film school and I was directing already.

My film aspirations had never gone away. But when you're in TV and when you're working on a show, I'm sure you're the same, there's no time for anything else. And I'm a terrible multi-tasker. I'd written a film that never got made, between *Fistful of Fingers* and *Shaun of the Dead* – called *Crawl* – about teenagers on a pub crawl. That was my attempt to do something in the vein of *American Graffiti* or *Dazed and Confused*, or the Kevin Smith film *Clerks* – something that was about young people, but quite kind of scatological and silly.

I'd written that script, and I had some interest in it... my agent liked it, but then I started doing TV stuff and that was a full-time job.

The thing is, whatever you're doing, the grass is always greener. You're always looking out the window at what other people are doing. In fact, I'd be looking at something like your film *Wonderland*, and thinking, 'What's he doing? He's shooting a film in London, I want to do that.'

It's funny, I thought about your film quite a lot recently, because my new film is shot in Soho, and the most recent one shot there before was *Wonderland*, and I remembered having seen it at the cinema, and reading an interview with you about the making of it. So there were a couple of times where we did one or two stolen shots, and whenever it would raise question marks with the crew, I'd say, 'Michael Winterbottom did a whole film like this!'

MW One of the TV shows you made was *Spaced* – which was great. It must have been exhausting to make?

EW Yeah, it was. It was at a budget level where there was no interference. Channel 4 just let us do what we want. Nobody really knew what it was going to be like, they just liked the performers and they thought the scripts were funny. It was basically – the show has to be 26-and-a-half minutes long, and you can say 'fuck' twice, but you can't say 'cunt'. Those were about the only guidelines we had.

I used to watch films like *Raising Arizona*, Sam Raimi's *Evil Dead II*, Jeunet and Caro's *Delicatessen* – and I would just watch those and think, 'Why don't more films look like this?' And the answer is: It's really difficult to do. When it came to doing *Spaced*, I was trying to do that style in comedy. And it's not easy.

MW You'd already worked with Simon Pegg. Was that the first time you'd worked with Nira Park, the producer?

EW I'd worked with Nira once before, briefly. We'd done some sketches with Matt and David for a Channel 4 sitcom weekend.

On *Spaced* there was a producer, a really nice creative guy, Gareth Edwards, who was great with the script, but he hadn't much filming experience. So I suggested Nira should come on board as a second producer who could run the day. And we've worked together ever since.

We did two series of *Spaced*, and at the end of the second one I was burnt out and I couldn't think about doing a third one. I felt I wanted to do something else – I wanted to make a movie. In a way I wanted to have a second chance at making my first movie. My debut had been so forgotten by everybody, it felt like I could pull the wool over people's eyes and make a first film again. Because *Spaced* was at Channel 4 we went to Film4 and developed the script with Paul Webster and Jim Wilson.

So immediately after *Spaced* finished in spring 2001, me and Simon sat down properly to write *Shaun of the Dead*, with Film4 and Nira producing, and we wrote the script over that summer, and we took it incredibly seriously – it looked like a screenplay, properly formatted, in the right font, and point size and everything.

MW That's very important.

EW Yeah, the right font, that's important. You can always tell when a script is an unsolicited script, it doesn't look right.

We had a kind of zombie episode in *Spaced* that was fun to make, so I said to Simon, 'I think we should do a horror-comedy, and we should try and find our own spin on it.' At first he was a bit reluctant, saying 'What is that? What is there to do, that isn't covered in Peter Jackson's films, or *Return of the Living Dead*?' So it was about finding a British response to those films. I remember we pitched it to Film4 as Mike Leigh's *Life is Sweet* meets *Dawn of the Dead*. The idea was that the horror element was straight and the characters were funny. So the comedy comes from the naturalism of the characters and their real responses. So there's nothing in *Shaun of the Dead*, aside from the zombies, that can't actually happen.

We had an office in [Berwick] Street, which we'd rented. We were like, 'We have to hire an office for two months and we have to go to the office every day and write the scripts.' That's what we did. I was making no money at this point, because I had turned down all the TV offers.

I remember being offered a TV drama show and saying to the producer, 'Hey, thank you so much for sending me this. I'm going to pass because I have this film script that I really want to do.' And they said something along the lines of, 'If I had a pound for every time I hear a director say that...'

I think a huge percentage of filmmakers in the UK never leave the kind of safety of doing TV, because they're scared a film might not happen.

I'd been a working TV director, and then for the next year I was not making any money, at all. I was doing the odd music video, but they didn't really pay much. Maybe if I got a commercial then that would keep me going for six months or something. There was a point where

I couldn't afford the rent on my flat anymore, I was going to have to move somewhere smaller and my landlord took pity on me and reduced my rent.

Then just when we finished the script, Film4 sort of stopped making films for about 18 months – they ran out of money. So now it's like, 'Oh no, now what?' Because Nira had a relationship with Channel 4, she managed to get them to put the *Shaun of the Dead* script in turnaround, so we could have it back, because otherwise it would have just been sitting there. So we got the script back, and then had the embarrassing task of going back to people we had had general meetings with before, but not partnered with and have to say, 'Hey, we're back again. We've got a script now.'

A lot of them gave us a really tough time. We went through second meetings with Pathé and the Film Council and – who else – Buena Vista, maybe? I remember the Film Council meeting was like, 'Why make this movie now?'

And I was worried I was going to become one of those people who's always talking about making a movie. And this is a thing Americans always say. That British filmmakers say, 'If I get my film off the ground', while Americans say, 'When I get my film off the ground'. So I was an 'if' person, and I felt like I was at the point where I was going to have to do something else. I was beginning to feel foolish for turning down other jobs.

And then we went to Working Title and I assumed because they were a mainstream behemoth they wouldn't be interested , but Eric said 'yes'. Without Eric Fellner there would have been no *Shaun of the Dead.*

MW In the last decade you've only really done one film in the UK. I know you've just done another. Were there other projects you wanted to do or was there always a pull to America?

EW I would love to have done more. I'm always envious of people that have more films in their filmography, like I always look at the Coen Brothers, and their work rate, and I always think 'Wow, those guys'. Then I think, 'Well, I guess there's two of them'.

The thing with the Coen Brothers is they are not sentimental about their work at all. They seem to make the films and move on very quickly. They're always looking forward and they never ever look back. They seem to do as little press as they possibly can, and then start making another movie. And that's the key to it. Whereas I feel like it takes a year to write and develop a movie, it takes a year to make it, and then there's a year promoting it. That was definitely the case with *Shaun of the Dead.*

After *Shaun* I did have Hollywood offers straight away, for much bigger films, but I felt it would be better to stay in the UK and make *Hot Fuzz.* It felt like the right thing to do, and I think it's probably one of the best decisions I ever made because now you see filmmakers make one independent film that has festival success and then they get sucked up into the blockbuster machine. And with that, I always feel that you never know what that person's second movie is.

I feel there's a lot of careers of writer-directors, or directors, that we don't really know who they are, who they might have become? I don't begrudge anybody who does that, but it does feel that there's been a generation of filmmakers lost to the sausage machine.

MW And presumably it is important that Nira is there being your own producer protecting your space. Because if you're just the director going into a massive studio film there would be very little protection?

EW In terms of having a bit of control, working with the same producer definitely helps. A lot of people make a mistake when they go to Hollywood and don't take their producer with them. I'd work with Nira on anything. We come as a pair. And Eric Fellner's produced all of my movies except for *Scott Pilgrim*, so now I want to work with these guys. And if I can't work with these guys, I'm not sure that I want to do it.

I've had two good Hollywood experiences – *Baby Driver* and *Scott Pilgrim vs. the World*, which is still, to date, my most expensive movie.

MW   It's very recognisably your movie. It's not an example of what you were saying about going into a studio and not hearing the director's voice.

EW   Yeah, I don't feel that I was compromised in the making of it. It was pretty out there. I don't think it would ever get made now. It was Universal who financed it – along with Working Title they had released *Shaun of the Dead* and *Hot Fuzz* – so there was some continuity in terms of some of the same execs, and that was definitely a help.

The project was brought to me by Universal and they were so excited I wanted to do this book that they owned. But then you get this weird thing where you have to kind of sell the movie back to them. I had to pitch back the movie that they'd asked me to make. It's quite strange when they say, 'So what is the movie exactly?' I said, 'Well it's an adaptation of the book that you sent me, which I've done to the best of my abilities.' And that happened again after we'd made the movie. They looked at it and said, 'So what is this exactly?' They were trying to find a box to put it in, where they could easily sell it, because it wasn't an easy sell.

One of the reasons that it's three years between movies is there was a solid year and a half of just trying to convince them to say, 'Yes'.

After *Scott Pilgrim* I knew definitely the next thing I did was going to be cheaper.

MW   Had you already written *World's End*, or did you come back and then start with Simon and Nick and Nira again on that?

EW   We had had the idea for it before *Scott Pilgrim*, but we hadn't written it. I'd been writing a couple of other things. Joe Cornish and I had worked on *Tintin* for Spielberg and Peter Jackson. And then the other thing I'd been planning from *Hot Fuzz* onwards was to make *Ant-Man* with Marvel and I was writing that. Joe Cornish and I had been working on a version of it since even before *Shaun of the Dead*. And then we finished a first draft after *Hot Fuzz*.

Then after *Scott Pilgrim* I wrote the first draft of *Baby Driver* because I'd done a two-picture deal with Working Title and Universal. That was the first thing that I'd written on my own.

I called Eric and I said, 'How would you feel if I told you the *Baby Driver* script is coming this week?' He says, 'I'll believe it when I see it, but I'm very excited.' And then maybe a day later I got an email from Nira, saying Eric is very ill and has cancer, aggressive bladder cancer and has a 50:50 chance of living.

So I talked to Simon and I said, 'We have to write *The World's End* right now, because we had promised Eric we would.' I think the fact that Eric was ill spurred me and Simon into action.

So I told the Marvel people, 'I have to go and write this other movie, it's important.' And me and Simon wrote *The World's End* in Eric's office, in Los Angeles, while he was getting better. It felt like it was the right thing to do, to make the movie we'd promised to make for Eric Fellner, and also to be back in the UK making a movie.

MW   And that's the last time you co-wrote with Simon? Was that because you just wanted to do different things?

EW   We never fell out. We always talk about writing something. But I think I definitely felt like I had something else in my system that I needed to get out.

In terms of collaborating it can be frustrating because whenever Simon's not doing something the phone will be ringing with him saying, 'Hey, we've got to sit down and start writing.' And then whenever I'm ready to write I'll be, 'Hey, I've got some time free if you want to brainstorm,' and he goes, 'Nah, I'm really busy on *Mission*.' So it always goes around like that.

And Simon is a brilliant writer but Simon is most interested in writing something that he's going to be in. If Simon's not going to be in it, why waste six months to a year writing something? So that limits the sort of things that I can do. And I was always a bit jealous of Simon and Nick, that as a writer-director, it would take me a minimum of three years to make a movie, but Simon could go off and shoot six movies in that time.

I wish I could make that many movies. Or at least one movie every two years. So there was an element there, with *Baby Driver*, where I said to myself, 'I have to go off and do my own thing.' *Baby Driver* was four years after *The World's End*, but that was because I was working on *Ant-Man*.

I had developed *Ant-Man* and after *The World's End* came out they said, 'Now it's happening'. I had a script that I'd written with Joe Cornish that I was very proud of. But as we were getting closer to actually shooting it became more of a committee process…

We were in Atlanta with sets being built, and we were getting notes on every draft and the same notes kept coming back. And Joe and I would go through the notes, there'd be ten notes, and we'd think, 'Okay four of these are fair, four of these I don't agree with, but I get it and we'll do them, and then these last two.' I would call them 'Jenga' notes, where if these changes are made, our version of the film is gone. So you'd go back and you think that you are compromising, you are being pretty compliant saying, 'Hey, so these eight notes are all good, these two we feel really strongly about.' You

The World's End (2013). (© Universal Studios/Working Title Films)

think you're playing ball, but you're not. Because they want you to change all ten.

So we basically reached an impasse.

I was on this scout and I saw Nira, and she said, 'I need to talk to you a second. They want us to fly back to Los Angeles, and have a meeting.' I knew that was serious. because we were actually in pre-production. And we went back to Los Angeles and they said, 'We've put the film on hiatus for a couple of weeks. We want to do a new draft with a different writer. We don't want you and Joe to do the new draft.'

I think I just said, 'Well, it's a shame, because I'm really proud of the script. But obviously there's an element where it's something different from what you guys want.' So rather than just walk off I said, 'Let's see the draft'.

So everybody went on hiatus. Every crew member went home, the stages are just sitting there, and what was supposed to be a two-week re-draft, which I wasn't allowed to be part of, stretched into six weeks, and I was in Los Angeles. So during that six weeks, I dusted off the *Baby Driver* script.

The *Ant-Man* script came in eight weeks later. By this time, in my head, I'd started to move on.

I woke up and Joe Cornish had sent me a text and he said, 'I've read the draft, call me when you've read it.' So I started reading and then I texted Joe and said, 'I'm 20 pages in, and already I don't want to do it.'

It was a shame as we felt we'd written something really good and that could work within their universe, but now it felt like it was buried under three coats of new paint.

I remember I said to my agent, 'As long as I'm making another movie by the time it comes out, I'll be fine.' And within about three months *Baby Driver* had been set up at another studio. But it was still a full year before it was green-lit, and that year was tough, because we were doing some casting and people are attached, but it's still not green-lit. And I remember, the lowest ebb was that by the time *Ant-Man* came out, *Baby Driver* still wasn't definitely happening.

I started to write other scripts, just in case it didn't happen. David Walliams and I wrote an animation film for DreamWorks – so I was getting paid and one was an adaptation that might still happen, maybe not directed by me, but it was an adaptation of a great book called *Grasshopper Jungle*.

I was feeling a lot of pressure and losing a lot of sleep and getting very kind of antsy, no pun intended, and I remember driving on Los Feliz Boulevard, near my house in LA, and being stuck behind a bus which had an *Ant-Man* advert on it. That was the first time I'd ever in my life actually been to a therapist. I'd never been until that point.

So when *Baby Driver* was green-lit, about three months later, it was such a blessed relief to be like, 'Okay, this is happening now'.

I'd come up with the idea for *Baby Driver* years ago, when I was first living in London. I just had this image of this car chase movie set to music. But back then I wasn't a director that could get anything made, I certainly couldn't get a car-chase film made, and also I knew that making a car-chase movie in the UK would be problematic.

MW Was your script set in Atlanta?

EW No, it wasn't, it was set in Los Angeles.

MW So you deliberately went back to exorcise your demons?

EW No, it was a tax-break thing. They gave me a list of the cities with good tax breaks and the choice was New Orleans, Atlanta, Cleveland, and Detroit. I went and scoped out all of them, and Atlanta was last on my list because of *Ant-Man*. But because of the time of the year Atlanta became the only option. And weirdly enough, as soon as I moved it to Atlanta and rewrote it for that city, I think it made the movie in a way.

Filmography

2004 *Shaun of the Dead*
2007 *Hot Fuzz*
2010 *Scott Pilgrim vs. the World* (US film)
2013 *The World's End*
2017 *Baby Driver* (US film)
2020 *Last Night in Soho* (Completed but not yet released)
2021 *The Sparks Brothers* (Documentary)

Steve McQueen

These are excerpts from a conversation that took place on 22 May 2020.

MW You made one film, *Hunger*, in the UK, but after that all your films have been set in the US. Why?

SM I had wanted to make *Shame*, my second picture, in London however, it was around this time that News International had been exposed for their phone-hacking practices. This made filming in the UK extremely difficult when it came to us researching the piece. No one wanted to speak to us in London, the trust just wasn't there, the doors were closed. So I spoke to Abi Morgan, the co-writer, and said, 'Abi let's go to New York'. New York, to me, has always been a place that's all about what you want, how you want it, 24 hours a day – therefore a perfect environment for this particular character and his story. Of course *12 Years a Slave* had to be shot in US, so that leaves us with *Widows*. *Widows* was an interesting one because where to set the piece came down to the type of criminality Lynda La Plante wrote about in her original story, where politics and crime are very closely intertwined. I felt this was something more embedded in the states and

Steve McQueen, on set, *Hunger* (2008). (Courtesy: Mary Evans/AF Archive/Film4)

Small Axe: Mangrove (2020). (© Turbine Studios/EMU Films/BBC/Amazon Studios)

nowhere exemplified this as much as Chicago. It had all the ingredients, politics, crime, issues around race, a huge FBI presence, and the likes of Mayor Daley. Chicago has always been about 'the deal'. What do I get? What's my cut? One of the most popular catchphrases in Chicago is, 'I got a guy'.

MW   You've just worked in Britain again. But this time you've made a TV series, *Small Axe*, for the BBC.

SM   Yes. Initially, *Small Axe* was conceived of as a TV series however, as soon as we got into the writers' room and began defining what stories we wanted to tell, it became clear the format had to be different. Each story needed to be a stand-alone film but, most importantly, exist as part of a collective. Which, in essence, is what *Small Axe*, which comes from an African proverb, 'If you are the big tree, we are the small axe' means.

It has been interesting to see the space this collection has occupied. Three of the films were debuted in cinemas during Film Festivals but have, of course, been shown on the streaming platforms along with television. It has been really interesting seeing them translate across all three.

MW   What period is it set in?

SM   It's set from '68 to '84.

MW   Did you have the idea and then work with a team of writers?

SM   Yes. Our starting point was wanting to tell stories, not about the wind rush generation, but their children. The people who were already established and interwoven into Britain and its culture. The Mangrove in Notting Hill functioned as a really interesting place to begin exploring this. To me, this piece has always been a western. It's about a guy called Frank Crichlow who says, 'Ok I want to make a legitimate cafe for West Indian people to come and congregate'. It then turns into a beehive for the aristocracy, rock stars, and of course local West Indians. Then when it gets onto the radar of the authorities, they aren't so keen on it. They saw it as a hub for black intellectuals who they perceived as dangerous and disruptive. So, like a Western, it's about a guy who opens up a saloon and the sheriff, who is sponsored by the state, keeps on hassling him. The story then morphs into something bigger when it is catapulted onto the front lines of civil rights in the UK.

MW   Is it one continuous story or is each episode its own story?

SM   Each film is its own story. We then go to a blues party for the second episode. These blues parties started because clubs didn't allow entry to Black people, or if they did there was a quota. So what did people do? They made their own clubs. I remember as a kid when you went to these house parties, it was complete magic, the music scented the air. All the films are about people making decisions for themselves when the British refused to make room for them. In many ways, the series is a rallying cry for others to do the same. Don't rely on whoever to do anything for you, make the space, create. Do it yourself.

MW   I'm interested you were so clear that it is cinema not TV, when it is being shown on TV. Do you feel there's a formal or aesthetic difference between the two? We've made stuff that has been financed by TV in the UK but shown as a cinema film abroad. So there doesn't seem to be that much difference.

SM   I first encountered cinema on TV, that was my entrance into it. So in this case, it doesn't matter where it is located, it is all about the intention of what one is trying to do.

MW   You've worked a lot with the cinematographer Sean Bobbitt who we worked with on *Wonderland*. That was his first film.

SM   Yes. *Wonderland* was the reason I wanted to work with him, I thought *Wonderland* was fantastic.

MW   He started with you on the short films – the video art.

SM   I don't make short films. I make artworks.

MW   I was struggling to think what the right word was.

SM   Well for me an artwork is about the intention of the medium, whatever endeavour one is participating in it becomes about what you do with it that ends up defining it. Context is everything. I worked with Sean on a film called *Western Deep*, which we shot in a South African goldmine. It's the deepest mine in the world at three-and-a-half kilometres underground.

MW   And when you made your first film, *Hunger*, was that a project that you specifically wanted to make as a film as opposed to an artwork? How did that come about?

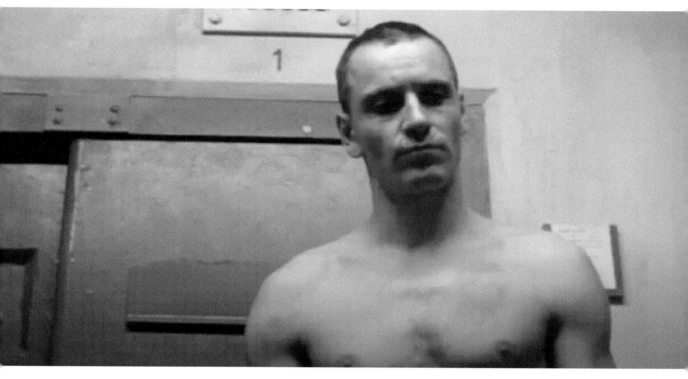

Hunger (2008). (© Blast! Films/Hunger Ltd)

SM   I think the subject dictates the form. I don't approach these things thinking, 'Is it a feature film? Is it a sculpture? Is it a photograph?'. I never want to impose myself too much on the subject, the subject imposes itself onto me. It shows me what it wants to be and how it wants to be presented, and *Hunger* needed to be a feature film. That's it really, it needed to be a narrative.

MW   How did *Hunger* come about? You had the idea for it and you took it to Iain Canning?

SM   No It was Jan Younghusband, she gave me £900,000 to make it. We also got money from the Northern Ireland Film Fund and Welsh Film Fund. I think in the end we got £1.3m, and we went and shot it. Iain came on board much later. *Hunger* was our introduction and immediately after that we made *Shame* together and then *Widows* sometime later. In the meantime, I worked with Plan B on *12 Years*. I think you've worked with Plan B?

MW   Yes. On *12 years*, did you have the idea and then take it to them?

SM   Well, Jeremy Kleiner at Plan B said, 'Look, I'm really interested in making a movie with you, do you have any ideas? I had been wanting to make a film about slavery for some time but hadn't quite found the story yet. I had been working with a writer but nothing was clicking. It was my wife, who is a historian, that said 'Why don't you research true stories?'. The next day we started looking and that very same day she said 'Look I think I've found it. It's this book called *12 Years a Slave*'. I read it and it was really quite incredible, as I had originally had this idea of a free black man who gets kidnapped, and lo and behold, what was *12 Years* about? On top of that, it read like a script. It really was crazy.

MW   There had been a TV version of it before. Did you ever watch that?

SM   It was a TV-film version and no I didn't watch it before. Amazingly I only heard about it after. It was made by Gordon Parks, an incredible man, an amazing photographer, journalist, and filmmaker. A renaissance man.

MW   A long time ago we worked with Tracey Emin on a film she made for the BBC – she made it through Revolution. I remember at the time, her saying she could have sold it as an artwork and got more money than the BBC had given her. She was frustrated about how the relationship worked between someone like her making a film for BBC, and how it would work if she was making it for a gallery.

I wondered how you thought those worlds compare, because British art seems incredibly vibrant in a way that British cinema doesn't?

12 Years a Slave (2013). (© Regency Entertainment (USA), Inc/LLC Bass Films/Monarchy Enterprises S.a.r.l.)

SM   The issue I see with British cinema is that there aren't enough young people. There is not enough imagination. I wouldn't have made a film if it wasn't for Jan Younghusband taking a chance on me. I just wouldn't be making films now. Certain film institutions are for certain people they believe can make films. More than likely, they would think people like me couldn't or shouldn't do it. I remember being laughed at for wanting to make a film. This kind of attitude creates a situation where people can't be experimental and the whole industry suffers because of it. Look at fashion, music, and art, we are pretty great at being inventive and creative there. But as soon as it gets to certain mediums that inclusiveness isn't allowed and therefore things become old and stuffy really quickly. I think it's all about access and possibility, isn't it?

MW   From your experience, what do you think are the factors that make the art world and fashion – but let's stick to the art world – much more open to the young, but also to experimental, difficult work that is also successful with the public?

SM   Because there is a market for it. Let's talk about music which is slightly more accessible, especially now the internet allows for young musicians to make and try things on their own. People are doing what they want, how they want, and to great effect. I think this sets a great example for how the film industry could, would, and should be. If you let young people tell their stories and create the things they want to it will refresh the industry for everyone. But sadly that isn't the case at the moment and the music industry allows for much more imagination and possibilities than in the film world. I think, in part, this is because there is always the question of 'who holds the purse strings' when you are making a film. I got in the back door. It wasn't Channel 4 or Film4 that supported me, it was Jan Young-husband, who was the maverick at Channel 4 Arts. She nearly lost her job for giving me that money, but when the awards started to come in everyone changed their minds.

MW   It seems, as an outsider, that the equivalent of BAFTAs for best films, is the Turner Prize. With the Turner Prize, when you look at the list of people – people who are doing complicated work – they have become well-known names, even to people who never go to galleries. But that is a prize specifically for British artists under 50. Whereas if you look at the BAFTAs, there have only been four films set in Britain, in the whole of the 21st century, that have won Best Film, and three of those films are period films and the only contemporary film was *The Queen*, about the royal family.

SM   Precisely. Who is making those films? Who are the type of people given access to that kind of investment and attention? The British film industry is going to die a terrible death unless people get real and invest in those who actually have stories to tell that reflect who we are today. There is obviously something terribly wrong. In fashion, art, and music you see people testing the temperature of the world around them, and in film, you just cannot. Obviously, there is something wrong.

Filmography

2011   *Shame* (US film)
2008   *Hunger*
2013   *12 Years a Slave* (US film)
2016   *Codes of Conduct* (US TV series: 1 episode)
2018   *Widows* (US)
2020   *Small Axe* (TV series: 5 episodes)

Lynne Ramsay

Lynne and I have met a few times – a long time ago – through a mutual friend, Alwin Kuchler. Alwin was the cinematographer on Lynne's two British films – *Ratcatcher* and *Morvern Callar*. Alwin then shot two films I made – *The Claim* and *Code 46*. These are extracts from a conversation which took place on 27 April 2020.

MW How are you?

LR Okay. I mean, you know, it's pretty challenging trying to work at home because our flat is quite small. I normally go to the office, but it's in Dalston, so I can't. I'm a bit of a hermit, so not much has changed in some ways, but I don't like not being able to exercise. I usually go swimming every day – so I'm really missing that.

MW You made your first two films in the UK, they had a lot of success. But you haven't worked here since. Is there a reason why you switched to America?

LR Well, it was just one of those things. In the case of *We Need To Talk About Kevin*, that book was only a bestseller here in the UK. I remember there was talk of making it in the UK, but it felt like a US film, you know, in terms of subject matter. You could've set it here, but there were so many

Lynne Ramsay, 2002. (Courtesy Mary Evans/AF Archive/Company Pictures)

things that just placed it there and it was written there. It's a great story and it's set in a specific place. I don't want to be completely tied to one country. I think you're a bit like that, as well, as a filmmaker.

MW   Did you live in America at one point?

LR   No. I mean you have to kind of live there when shooting. But that's all really.

MW   When did you get involved in *We Need To Talk About Kevin*?

LR   I got the material through my agent, Jenne Casarotto, she met Lionel [Shriver – the author], and as soon as I read it, I was like, 'I want to do this'. I think that a lot of people were quite frightened. The BBC people had read it and were like 'Oh, this is too dark.' Some people just found it a wee bit scary, maybe, to go there. So basically I said to Jenne, 'I want to do it', and then I went to the BBC and said, 'I want to do it', and then they got involved because they were like, 'Okay, if you've got a vision of it then we'll go with it'. So, I didn't get a producer involved until much later on.

MW   So you were your own producer, in a way.

LR   Yeah, yeah. Pretty much. I was on the project for a few months, maybe a year, before getting anyone else involved, and then there was a producer that Tilda Swinton recommended, when she came on board, who had worked on *Michael Clayton*. And because we were New York-based I thought it would be better to get someone who was based there, and then she got pregnant just when we were about to shoot, so it passed over to Luc Roeg, you know, Nic Roeg's son.

MW   Yes, I know Luc.

LR   I think a lot of people had passed on it. Because it was written in the form of letters so it wasn't easy to adapt… It was also over 400 pages – it was massive – so people were like, 'It's not really makeable'. That was before it became a bestseller or it won any prizes. I was lucky to get it that early on. I think the attraction was that I'd never seen anything about that subject matter, about a mother who doubts her love for her son... you know, it was quite a taboo subject matter. I think a lot of the thoughts that are in it are thoughts that people have, but never tell anyone. It had this really interesting battle of wits between this mother and son, that I thought was amazing. But it was no mean feat to get that made into a film because of the form of it.

MW   How long was your scriptwriting process?

LR   Probably a year-and-a-half. It was a mad script to write, because it had all these timelines going on and I don't really like flashbacks in the traditional sense, so it was a real challenge. And then I got a weird phone call from somebody, the script had leaked out, I don't know how, but my dad was dying at the time, and I got this phone call saying – Summit wants to do it. You can have this amount of money, and it can be any actors you want, stuff like that. So they seemed to be really, genuinely going to do it.

So I was in New York prepping just before the financial crash, I was crewing up and seeing actors and stuff like that, and then there was the crash and everything got put on the back burner and Summit were like, 'We just want to concentrate on *Twilight*'.

I just felt 'I need to cut this script and make it work for a certain budget, because I put all this work into it...'

So I spent maybe another six months cutting it.

MW   What was the budget?

LR   I think when the Summit people came in they were talking about around $10 million, or something. After Summit pulled out, I think it ended up about six or something like that? Which is still pretty good, but, you know, if you shoot in America – I'm sure you know this – it's quite expensive.

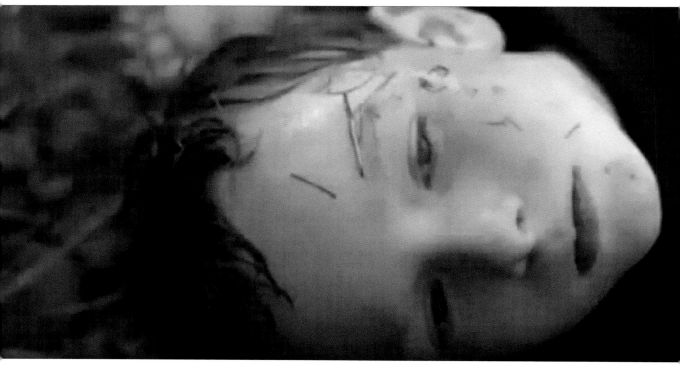

Ratcatcher (1999). (© Pathé Fund Limited/Les Productions Lazennec)

When I was shooting, it was basically me and the line producer in New York, so it was a bit of a strange process in that respect. I think you end up becoming a producer in some respects, the more you direct. I don't know if you find it like that?

MW Yeah. But then it's nice to have a partner – so you've got a bit of head-space, you don't have to worry about all that stuff.

LR Yeah, definitely. I've worked with some really good people, but, then you need to meet new people. I think I'm always looking for that producer.

MW From my point of view, it seems a shame, and strange – that you've only made two films in the UK... Does it seem like that to you? Have there been other films you wanted to make here?

LR There's been a ton of stuff. It's funny when people say 'you've only done a few films', because I wish I'd made more. Obviously, there are some things that I spent a couple of years on that didn't happen for various reasons, and then you've got other ideas that you want to make but...

MW Such as?

LR I was involved with *The Lovely Bones* for a while.

MW Was that another book you got before it was published? Through your agent.

LR No, that one was through Jim Wilson, actually. He was working at Film4 and he thought it was interesting. I was sent, maybe the first three or four chapters, not the whole thing, and I thought there was something super interesting there. But then it was much later that the book came out and became a really massive bestseller in the States, and it was a strange thing where it felt more and more like what I was doing with the book wasn't really what people really wanted. There was just much more pressure to make it exactly like the book, which I didn't think was going to work. I wanted it to be a loose adaptation. So reluctantly I just backed out of that. It was a bit crazy, I've been in a few crazy ones, it's just a crazy kind of industry. But I did a lot of work on it and learned a lot of stuff from that experience.

I should've made more though. But writing is a long process if you're trying to get to the bottom of something. I think it's where you do all the prep for the film really, it's the time I visualise the film.

There was another one – I was prepping it and they wanted to change the whole thing.

MW Was that *Jane Got A Gun*?

LR Yeah.

MW Your agent at the time was Chris Donnelly, wasn't he? He was my agent as well.

LR Yeah, I mean Chris was, you know, his wife died, so that was all happening. It was a bit of a nightmare for both of us to be honest. But the prep was amazing, and I'd cast the film, cast the extras and things like that, so it's almost like you've made the film… It's like being a chef a bit, I suppose, once you've done the prep – that's quite a lot of the movie. So you learn quite a lot. I'd never worked with guns, or horses and stuff like that. Unfortunately that one got away,

MW How did you get involved in that film?

LR I got sent a script, it was by a young writer, I think he was only 21, and I normally always write my own stuff but I thought it had real potential. It was a really amazing opening and idea.

So I wrote a draft, and I thought it was pretty kickass.

MW And you went and got Natalie Portman involved, is that how it worked?

LR No. They had developed the script through her company, so they were looking for a director. And it was a good script. But I think once the financiers got involved, it produced a different vibe in the whole thing. It didn't work out.

MW Were there other ideas after *Morvern Callar*, other UK-set films that you thought about?

LR I wrote a kind of post-*Ratcatcher* thing which was based on the kid, but grown-up, and that was called *Rocking Horse*. It was actually a comedy but a dark, twisted one, as you can imagine. And I still have that script, which then I started wondering whether I could make it into a series or something. So I wrote that. I put it to one side – but it's always been there in the background. And then there was a couple of other things, but mainly I think it was *The Lovely Bones* which took the longest. We were on that a couple of years – me and my friend Liana Dognini [who co-wrote *Morvern Callar*] – she died, you know, unfortunately. And we'd been working on *The Lovely Bones* together… We just felt we were handing in endless drafts... Where it wasn't quite like the book that everyone knew and loved at that point. So, that was frustrating for a while.

I've got one of those folders – I'm sure you do too – full of ideas that are really cool, but just didn't get made somehow.

MW What are you working on at the moment?

LR I'm working on two scripts. There's one that I am a bit stuck on – just because it's really massive – well, it's not a massive project, but it's got a lot of big ideas in it. It's based on an ice photographer and it's a period piece set at the turn of the century, 1890, so it's a completely different thing for me.

So I've got 75 pages of that. And there's one I'm co-writing. It is from a Margaret Atwood short story. That's exciting as well – because you're working from such a tiny text... But, normally, I do one thing at a time.

I haven't worked on two things at the same time before, so that's a big deal for me, and I think there's a kind of chomping at the bit to get started. And I was really quite enjoying the development process and feeling like these things were getting quite near to being made before this [Covid-19 lockdown] kicked in. I wasn't in prep or anything like that, like some people I know, so thank the gods for that.

MW Are they set in the UK?

LR One is set in the Arctic and one in Alaska. Maybe it's remote enough to actually get a crew!

MW It's interesting that you're thinking about TV. You've not done that before?

LR There's been some interesting stuff sent to me, but it's better if you come up with your own ideas, if you devise it yourself. I've got an idea that would be set in Glasgow. But it's early days with that. I'm actually speaking to a writer. He's from New York. I think I'm a bit more open to writing with other writers now, rather than getting stuck in a feature-film script forever, on my own. It's a bit isolating. I've had these ideas and I've not been doing anything with them and I thought, 'Right, let's just try to brainstorm this a little bit.' What about you? Are you going to make more UK-based things?

MW   I don't know. I'd like to make films about ordinary life in Britain. But it feels like those stories are bound to be for TV. And now maybe that space has gone, even on TV. You know, it feels like the BBC wants to be Netflix…

LR   Yeah, I totally agree with that. It's a weird one, because maybe the smaller stories you might have seen, would've been an art-house film in the Nineties. Sometimes on TV you watch stuff and they start off really well, you're interested, and then when it gets to the umpteenth episode… you're just cooking while you're watching it, you're not really engaging.

MW   Is there a key producer that you've worked with, or has it been a different group of people each time?

LR   It's been different people… I think I've always had a dream to have the same producer for that continuity. But unfortunately it hasn't always happened like that, you know. I really enjoyed working with Robyn Slovo on *Morvern Callar*, but then she was off doing something else… I talk about working with Robyn again, Jim [Wilson] and I are involved in another project, and then I've met this really interesting documentary producer called Jocelyn Barnes… But I think maybe part of this whole conversation is that, I have, I think, become the producer myself in some ways.

I think lately I've found that you have to be the master yourself, in a sense. You do need to take on a role as a producer as well as a director, in a way that I didn't think when I first started. And I don't always want to do that, but I've found you have to. Especially if you go to a TV company. I'd rather have the whole thing ready and then maybe involve a producer that I choose myself. Rather than go down the director-for-hire route that I'm sure you wouldn't go down either.

MW I have a company, Revolution – so we tend to develop our own stuff and then go out and try and get the money to make it. But I decided to stop working for a few months – just before the lockdown – and I was immediately offered a couple of TV shows, but it was like – 'Can you start next week?'. They'd done all the development, written all the scripts, got all the actors, and then it was like, 'Who shall we get to direct?'

LR Oh my God, that's mad.

It's just a windy road sometimes – filmmaking. I've had a lot of things that haven't come to anything, but they often lead to other things – or, what doesn't kill you makes you stronger.

MW Or just tired.

LR Or tired. I suppose we've just got to be optimistic about doing our best stuff, and that people want to see it.

Filmography

1999   *Ratcatcher*
2002   *Morvern Callar*
2011   *We Need To Talk About Kevin*
2017   *You Were Never Really Here*

Stephen Daldry

These are excerpts from a conversation that took place on 15 May 2020. Stephen was in New York. I had met Stephen a few times before, at a film festival, or in a bar. But the last time was probably at least 10 years ago.

MW How is New York?

SD It's a bit like the zombie apocalypse, you know. The streets are empty, the rubbish isn't being cleared up. The only people around, really – after curfew – are people off their heads on crack or something... so they move very slowly. So it feels very weird, without people, without animation – it doesn't feel like a pretty city.

MW Are you allowed to go out?

SD Yeah. It's not as strict as Paris. Or even London. You can move around. You've got to wear masks everywhere.

MW Your first three films were made in Britain and were all very successful – and then for a dozen years you haven't made any films here in Britain. Is that for purely personal reasons, or were there other factors involved, push or pull factors?

SD It's nothing to do with Britain whatsoever. There are personal reasons. I mean, just where one's point of interest is. Just talking generally, choosing which film to make is so hard, I find it really difficult. It's

Stephen Daldry on the set of *The Crown* (2016/17). (photo: Robert Viglasky)

like a love affair, isn't it? You know, you've got to fall in love with somebody and you're going to be in love with them for many years. I'm sure that other directors work in a more coherent way, but I tend to flirt. You tend to flirt with projects and you fall in love a little bit. But then you get to a certain point and you go, 'No, I don't think this is for the long term'. Do you know what I mean? 'I don't think I can sustain this relationship', that's going to have to be sustained for at least two years, sometimes more than two years.

I mean the awful thing about me is, I know I tend to be a bit of a butterfly when it comes to projects. I settle on one and see whether I might like its pollen, and then I go bouncing off if I don't. And that can be frustrating, I know, for people who are trying to get me to make those films, because I can spend quite a lot of time exploring whether I want the relationship, before I decide that I don't want the relationship.

At certain times you can make a decision quite fast. There was a point in my life where I wanted to try to do things that I don't know how to do. So, for example, an opportunity came up to do a film in Brazil, so I spent a year in Brazil doing a film in Portuguese, a language I didn't speak, working with people who not only didn't speak English, but couldn't read or write. And that just felt so impossible. Because they can't read, so there's no script, you've just got to improvise each day in a language that you don't know how to speak, with people who are challenged in all sorts of ways, to do with sleep deprivation and drugs, and in a context that's incredibly hard for them to live, let alone try to make a movie.

And that was fantastic.

We moved into this favela and it took a year of my life, and the film played in Brazil but didn't really play anywhere else in the world, but I loved the time I spent there. It's one of the great joys of the job we have, exploring avenues or cultures or ideas or themes, that you can explore for such a long time, and invest so much time of your life. You have the resources to say, 'I'm going to go and live with three kids in Brazil, for however many years, and make a film about them' – which is sort of amazing.

MW You said that was all improvised, but there was a Richard Curtis script as well. Was that just a story outline?

SD   Yeah, it was a story outline. Because the kids couldn't read. So obviously it was a bit frustrating for Eric Fellner when he came to visit the set and was going, 'I don't understand where you are in the script,' and we said, 'We're not really doing the script, Eric. We're just following our nose and seeing what they can come up with.' And there were days with that group when we couldn't film because the kids were too tired, or there'd been a gun fight where they live. We tried to house them, but it was very complicated. You know what it is like better than anyone. The opportunity to film was not always there. You would have to find the right circumstances in which you could turn over. But I loved it. It was one of the great journeys of my life

But I don't feel I've ever really been away from London, I suppose because I do so many plays there.

I did a play with Pete Morgan called *The Audience*. And I really enjoyed that and then at the end of doing that play in London, we had to do it again in New York.

Then Pete and I had a conversation saying, 'Do we think we've got anything else to say on this story?', which is about the royal family in post-war Britain and we went, 'Yeah, okay, well let's pitch it to Netflix as a TV show.'

So we pitched it to Netflix, and then you spend three years of your life in London doing *The Crown*.

MW   What stage did you come onto *Trash*? Was that something that Eric had developed and then came to you?

SD   No, there was a book by an English teacher. It's a kids' story. He had worked in Brazil and Manila, so we had to choose one or the other. Manila didn't really have a film industry, so it felt a bit easier to set it in Brazil. Then we asked Richard to help us work out what the story might be.

But you spend – I don't know whether you do this – but I spend years sometimes on shows that I never actually get to do. There are quite a few that I've spent huge amounts of time and money on. And then what happens is that I get to a point where I decide I don't have anything to say about the story, or the story doesn't really yield anymore to me, or I don't know how to do it...

There was one instance where the studio who wanted to make it decided it was too expensive. But that's only ever happened to me once. Most of the time, it's me going, 'I don't want to do it anymore'.

The most expensive, the most ridiculous one, was *Everest*. Which, in the end, Tim Bevan carried on and made some years later, at Working Title. Stacey Snider was running Universal at the time and I managed to persuade Stacey to give me three-and-a-half million dollars to mount an expedition to climb Mount Everest. So I spent four-and-a-half months, and three-and-a-half million bucks, climbing Mount Everest, with a whole team and an IMAX camera, and doing the whole thing.

MW   Was the idea to shoot plates? What was the point? Was it for research or for shooting?

SD   Well, I wanted to experience it. And to shoot plates.

MW   What happened?

SD   Jon Krakauer had written a book about the disaster in '96 called *Into Thin Air*. And I was really keen on the story. I'd spent a lot of time in Kathmandu. I'd met everybody who'd survived – I mean this is years of work – I was fascinated with how Jon Krakauer approached it. We got different screenplays written.

I don't know how much you know about mountain climbing, but you've got to spend a lot of time up Mount Everest to acclimatise. So we went to Base Camp, and then you've got to keep going up and down the mountain to acclimatise to the different heights. This is what I did. Then after quite a few months of doing this, I sort of went, 'I don't know whether this is worth it. The view isn't that good, and I'm frozen.'

In the end it's a story about hubris. I kept on battling with this problem with the story. You have these people, these rich people, who are climbing Mount Everest, and they are struggling and then they die and you sort of go, 'Well, that'll teach them, won't it?'

I never got beyond that. I don't think you can make a film about hubris. I just couldn't find my way through it, so I withdrew.

That was the most expensive one. Then there was *Kavalier and Clay*, I don't know whether you know the book? I spent a lot of time developing that with Scott Rudin, but in the end Paramount didn't want to pay for it. We spent too much. Our pitch must have cost six million bucks. It was the most expensive pitch.

MW Really?

SD It's a book about the start of comic books in the Second World War. And we decided that we would do a very complicated pitch. We took over a warehouse in New York and we created different worlds that you could enter, because a lot of the film was animation. We commissioned animation companies around the world to create demonstrations of animation. Then we must have created five floors of different worlds you could enter. It was like a show, but a very expensive show where you would get into the world of *Kavalier and Clay*. And in the end Brad Grey who was running Paramount didn't really buy it. I also wanted to use a couple of actors who were unknown at the time – Andrew Garfield and Ben Whishaw – and they just went, 'We need stars. We don't know who these people are.'

We're trying to turn it into a TV show now.

Another one was the *Battle of Britain*. I spent a lot of time with Eric on that. I'm fascinated with the Battle of Britain, and Spitfires. And I used to fly – I went to university on a RAF scholarship, so I persuaded Eric that if I was going to do it, what I really needed to do was learn how to fly a Spitfire. So I spent months taking Spitfire flying lessons. And I loved it. It was the best time.

Then in the end you go, 'Oh well, that was great. I'm not sure I want to make the film anymore, but it was great.' But those explorations, you must do it, you have vast explorations into worlds or ideas that you then, somehow, for whatever reason, you don't feel like you can take them to the point where you can sit for another two years and make the movie. You have the love affair and then you finally realise that you don't feel you can settle down with them.

MW   Was there a specific story, or a script, on the Battle of Britain film?

SD   There was a story. Basically it was about the women who flew the Spitfires to put them in the right place to be flown. Women pilots. It's not a very well known story. It was about class – and saving the country

The other thing is, whenever you do a play, people always want you to do a movie of it. Sometimes it works, like turning *The Audience* into *The Crown*. With *Billy Elliot* it went the other way. It was Elton who wanted to make it into a musical. I sat on that for a long time and Elton carried on pushing, saying 'I've got a new song, I've got a new song'. In the end we made it and I thought the stage show was better than the film.

Now Eric wants to turn it back from a stage show into a movie. I'm like, 'Have I got the energy?' With some stories you just feel, 'Well I've done that. I need a new adventure. I need a new love affair.'

MW   The two producers you've worked most with are Scott Rudin and Eric Fellner. Do you develop stuff with them?

Billy Elliot (2000). (© Tiger Aspect/Working Title Films/BBC Film)

SD   With the play *The Inheritance* Eric came and said, 'Can we do it as a TV
      show?' So Eric will do the work and we'll see if we want to do it as a TV
      show. But sometimes I feel, does everything have to continue? Can't
      you just make something, and then move on to the next thing? You

tend to get a piece of work that goes on for years because you're still working on the same story.

I'm trying to think when we did *The Audience*, the play. It must have been five years ago. We're still doing it. We're still basically doing the Queen meets prime ministers, and it's been five years. We're still doing that fucking show. It's different, and it's interesting, and I'm not knocking it, but it's amazing how hard it is to move onto new projects because the old ones keep going.

MW   Did Peter [Morgan] bring *The Audience* to you, or were you involved from the inception?

SD   Pete was leading on the play. Pete said, 'I want to do a play about the Queen and her prime ministers.' So we did workshops. At one point Pete was like, 'Do I want to do this because I've already done the film *The Queen*?'

I was really interested in the prime ministers, because I thought we could use them to do a show about post-war Britain. And I was interested in the idea that you could create a head of state who was slightly left of centre. It's not a true depiction of her.

But, if it was Helen Mirren, people would believe that was actually what the Queen thought, that she had a slightly left-of-centre point of view. I think that people did buy into that. They think that she is one nation, and they believe she loves Africa, and she's not racist… all the things that we project onto her. I don't think they're true, but people sort of bought it. And they carry on buying it in the TV show. I like the idea of trying to shift the country left of centre, by pretending that is where the Queen is.

MW   Or you could see it as making the monarchy more popular by pretending she's left of centre.

SD   But I think that's interesting. The more left of centre you make her, the more popular she is.

MW You've been making *The Crown* for TV. Do you think there has been a shift of resources to TV from film?

SD We thought we had a lot of material. And it was very early on in Netflix, hardly anybody worked there, it was six people and a photocopier. What we asked for was quite outrageous actually. We said, 'You have to decide in the meeting. You've got one hour, but then we're going to another meeting. So you have to say, in this meeting, if you want it. No, "Oh, we'll call you in a week", Say now, "yes" or "no".' And after 40 minutes, they said, 'Yeah, alright. We'll do it. You don't need to go to another meeting, you can stay with us.'

At the cost of hundreds of millions of dollars. So that's what we did. And we stayed with them and they've been very nice ever since

MW How many episodes have you directed?

SD I did two in season one, two in season two. I didn't do any in season three because I was busy with my plays.

MW With *Billy Elliot*… how did that come about? Were you involved in the development?

SD Lee was an old friend, so he sent me the script and then Eric came on board. But it was a very little film, no one really cared about it. And I didn't know what I was doing, so it didn't really matter, the stakes were incredibly low, which I think was an advantage for us. It was cheap, and the stakes were low. I don't think anybody really liked it when we finished it. That was a real surprise hit.

But don't forget, you know, so much of my life is devoted to the theatre. I love doing theatre, and the two are incredibly different. I mean, film is so much harder, in lots of ways.

MW In what ways?

SD Well, it's much more lonely.

MW Lonely? That's interesting.

SD   Because in the theatre, everyone can see everything that's made all the time. And the people you start with are the people you end with. With film it's like a relay race. The people you start with aren't the people you shoot with, and they aren't the people you finish with, and they aren't the people you release with.

MW   With *The Hours* and *The Reader*, did you read the book and then develop the film?

SD   With *The Reader*, I read the book and wanted to do it, but Anthony Minghella owned the rights. He'd bought it years ago. And he wanted to write the adaptation, so I had to go to Anthony and say, 'You've got to give it to me and I'll do it with David Hare'. In the end Anthony was very gracious and said, 'It will take me some years to get to it', so he gave it to me, as long as he and Sydney Pollack would produce it. Then both Sydney and Anthony died during filming. Which was a little bit catastrophic because the other part of the deal was, 'If I do it with you, Anthony and Sydney, I don't want any interference from Harvey who funds your company.' I never had a problem with Harvey on a work front, but I just didn't want him to have final cut. And Anthony and Sydney had assured me that would be the case, and then they both died. So then I was stuck with Harvey.

MW   Did he try and interfere?

SD   Of course. But it was a good battle and we got through it.

With *The Hours* Scotty had the book and he had already started talking to David Hare.

MW   Would you have liked to make more films? Does that bother you?

SD   For five years, I've been trying to work out how to do *Wicked*, the musical, as a film.

Working on the scripts. Trying to figure it out, you know. That's a love affair that actually has sustained, because I don't know how to do it. And that's sustained over years. And then I've got a load of theatre stuff I'm meant to be doing when the theatres reopen – if they reopen – which I'm working on. And a few shows for Netflix which are in different stages of development. I'm spending quite a lot of time on a lot of projects, I don't know which one's going to settle with me, or settle with anybody else. We just have to see.

MW   You normally develop several things at the same time?

SD   Yeah. It's usually people I know saying, 'Do you think there's a way through on this?' or, 'Are we interested in this?' And you go, 'Well yeah, maybe. Maybe'. And then you've got to go through a process of going, 'Yeah. Yeah. Yeah. Yeah', trying to avoid the inevitable, 'No, I'm not really'. Without wasting too much time, or too much of anybody else's time, and too many resources.

MW   But it does take a lot of time though, doesn't it?

SD   It takes forever. Everything takes forever. People give you scripts to read and you go, 'Oh no, don't. It'll take me forever.'

I find everything takes me two years. A play will take me two years, a film will take two years, minimum. If I don't feel I've got something to say, then it's probably best to shut up. I don't have to do another show – I can do something else. I can go and build something. And I like building things, so I get lost in building, in construction projects, because I really like construction projects.

MW   Like what? Is this a metaphor for the plays or is this an actual construction project?

SD   No, it's construction projects. Building things. I'm involved with a pier, rebuilding a pier here in New York, in the Hudson river. And I love doing it. It's a park. I love the idea of building a park, it's great. Building theatres, I've always liked building theatres.

With films you've got to have a real reason for doing them, because it's just so long. Unless you really fall in love. Which is why I think I'm a problem because I do butterfly around different projects, and test them out, and test them out. And then go, 'No, I don't want to do it'. I think people do get frustrated with me. They go, 'Well you spent all that time on it, and all that money on it, and now you don't want to do it.' And I go, 'No, I don't want to do it anymore.'

Filmography

2000   *Billy Elliot*
2002   *The Hours*
2008   *The Reader*
2011   *Extremely Loud & Incredibly Close* (US film)
2014   *Trash*
2016   *The Crown* (TV series: 4 episodes)

Ben Wheatley

These are excerpts from a conversation that took place on 30 April 2020.

MW   I know you set up Rook Films. So maybe that's a good point to start. Why did you want to have your own company?

BW   I remember reading an interview with New Order and someone said, 'Why do you play in the unique way that you play?' And they said, 'Oh because that was the way we learnt our instruments. We didn't know any other way of doing it.' I think that's true of us. When we started, with *Down Terrace*, the first film I made, we didn't know anybody in the industry really, and we didn't know how to do anything, so we had to do it all from scratch. So we made up our own way of working from there. Rook Films comes out of that.

It seems to me the best way of making stuff, the most efficient way, is originating it and then producing it and financing it yourself. We see it through from the beginning to the end. All the way out to the sales and stuff. It's only in recent times I've started working with other production companies really, and that has its own advantages and disadvantages. But the simplest way of making stuff is definitely making it yourself.

MW Before you did *Down Terrace*, you'd been doing a couple of seasons of *Ideal* with Baby Cow.

BW Yeah. I'd been doing a lot of ads and I did an in-house BBC thing called *Wrong Door*. I did the live action stuff for *Modern Toss*, for Channel 4. It was interesting doing those things.

The way we ended up making the film was that, when we were doing *Ideal*, I was trying to do some drama, and they basically said, 'You can't do drama if you've done comedy. You're not a drama director.'

And it blew my mind, and I went to my agent and said, 'What am I going to do?' And he said, 'You've got to make a short film and that'll convince them that you can do drama.' And I thought, 'Fucking hell, really? A short film? I don't want to do that.'

So we made *Down Terrace* off the back of that. But I still couldn't get a meeting within the BBC even after I'd made that film and it had been a success.

When I started on the film stuff there was still a bit of money left in it. Film4 was still making stuff. BBC Film were making stuff. So once you'd made something you could plug into that.

MW What was the budget on *Down Terrace*?

BW Six grand. It was three lots of two grand – I put in two grand, Rob Hill put in two grand, and Andy Starke, the producer, put in two grand. In the end the film cost £25k, but only because we were stupid and we put some licensed music in it.

MW Post costs would have been on top of that though?

BW No, because we all came from a post background. So we mastered the film as well, we did the whole lot. And I blagged bits of post as well so… that was the real money. That was how much it cost us. Obviously there are deferred payments and all that stuff, so it's a bit of a con, the number is massaged slightly, but on *Down Terrace* we did pay

Ben Wheatley, 2017. (photo: Antonio Olmos)

A Field in England (2013). (© Rook Films Limited/Channel Four Television Corporation)

everybody afterwards – and the crew worked on every film after that as well. They're people I've been working with for 10... 12 years now.

MW Did you make money from the film? Who released it?

BW Metrodome. We took 20 grand for an MG [Minimum Guarantee]*. I think we had an American MG as well. So with the two MGs we paid off all our deferments. But the film needs to make ten to fifteen times the MG before it can go into profit. It was successful for me in terms of opening the door into making movies.

MW And then it was *Kill List*. How did you fund that one?

---

* A 'minimum guarantee' is a flat fee that the distributor agrees to pay a producer for the rights to distribute a completed film, independent of whether the film is successful, or not.

BW That was through Film4. It cost about £700,000. There was an initiative that they had through Warp and through Studio Canal. After I'd made *Down Terrace*, I wrote three scripts immediately – a cheap one, a middle one, and an expensive one. And we pitched all three and they obviously went for the cheap one, which was *Kill List*. That was the one that we could have made ourselves, if we'd got no money.

MW And the middle and expensive ones?

BW God, I can't remember. I think the middle one was a comedy which almost got made again later on, but didn't. The expensive one might have been *Freak Shift*, which is the sci-fi we've been trying to get made for ages.

MW You have your own company, you have your own space, you've kept control. But on low-budget films don't you find it hard to cover the costs of a company?

BW No. We don't have any costs.

MW That helps.

BW We've never had any costs. I had a company in the Nineties that went bust, and it was so awful, and I realised it was because we had overheads. So if we never have any overheads then you can't really ever go bust. So we've never had an office, we've never had any staff, we never have development people.

When we did *High-Rise* with Jeremy Thomas, Amy [Jump] just went in and went, 'I don't want any money to write the script, I'll write the script, and then if you like it, you can make it, and if you don't then we can all just walk away.'

MW I imagine Jeremy Thomas liked that?

BW Yeah, he did. He was surprised. But it also means you don't have to get any notes. The development stuff is a lot easier – because you don't have to do it. No one can really tell you anything.

MW Was *Sightseers* the same basic formula as *Kill List* in terms of the financing?

BW Yeah. *Kill List* was Rook, partnered with Warp. And *Sightseers* was Rook partnered with Big Talk. There was already a script they'd been developing for many years. And I felt like making a comedy after making *Kill List*. I wanted to make something that was less miserable. So I took it. I didn't even really read the script because I knew Alice and Steve, so I thought, 'Fuck it, I'll do it. That sounds like it could be a good laugh.' I wrote a treatment saying there was going to be a lot of improvisation and I got the job on that premise really. And then Amy rewrote it totally.

MW Do you improvise on set a lot?

BW It depends. *Sightseers* was a massive amount of improvisation – there were about 120 hours of rushes – which may seem small to you…

MW About average.

BW Yeah, so that was a lot of improv. You'd improv into the scene and out of the scene, and sometimes the scenes would go on for half an hour and you'd just follow them around doing stuff. So that was probably the purest improvisational film I've done. *Kill List* was more… I'd seen how *The Thick of It* had been made – that idea of doing sort of paraphrases of the script – and I liked that a lot, so I started doing that. It takes the edge off bad scripts really. So *Kill List* was paraphrased. *Down Terrace* was paraphrased. But in the end both of them were quite close to the scripts. *Sightseers* was on and off the script, though the funniest lines were mainly script, but then a lot of other funny stuff made it in as well. Then *A Field in England* and *High-Rise* were very much on the script. Amy's script was too good and there was no point messing around with it. *Free Fire* was a bit of both.

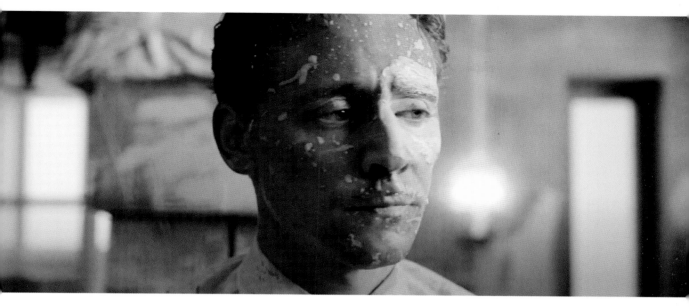

High-Rise (2015). (© RPC High-Rise Limited/BFI/Channel Four Television Corporation)

MW And since *A Field in England* has it just been Rook, or do you still partner up with different people?

BW Well, *High-Rise* was RPC on its own. And obviously *Rebecca* has been with Working Title. But *Kill List, Free Fire* and *Colin Burstead* were just straight Rook Films.

MW I talked to Peter Strickland and you produced one of his films?

BW In the loosest terms. I was an exec on his film and I found it really uncomfortable. I'm certainly not going to tell Peter how to direct a film or give him notes, because I think it's fucking rude to give notes.

MW That's the best sort of executive producer.

BW *Down Terrace* was just an anomaly. I'd been talking about making a film for 10 years or 15 years, and not getting it together and Andy had been the same and Rob Hill had been the same. So we finally pulled our arses out of the mud and did it. I felt like my voice wasn't being represented, so I made a film that I felt was true to the environment that I'd grown up in.

Kill List was my go at making a horror film. I basically just tried to make something that was made out of my own nightmares... I thought if it could scare me then it could scare other people.

A Field in England was more of a reaction to the fact we hadn't got some other bigger film made.

MW What was the budget on *A Field in England*?

BW It was £300k in the end. But what had happened was we went to make the film and Film4 went, 'Oh, you're making a film are you?' and we went, 'Yeah, yeah. You want to come in on it?', and they're like, 'Oh yeah, that sounds good'.

MW So they put in the whole 300?

BW Yeah.

MW It's a beautiful film. Which was the big film that didn't get made?

BW *Freak Shift*, which is a sci-fi film that we've been trying to make for a few years. We almost got the money, but we just didn't quite get enough. So I said, 'Right, I'll step away from it'. After that we managed to very quickly reorganise. I didn't want a year to go by without having done anything, so we made *A Field in England*.

Colin Burstead was a similar thing. I don't think anyone would have been interested in that story if I had asked to develop it. But at that point we had some money left over from *Free Fire* so we could just do it. It was the first film since *Down Terrace*, where we cut it and we watched it back and went, 'Oh, it's done. That's it.' No conversations with anybody. That was really refreshing. Then we sent it to people we knew at BBC and they really liked it. And then we had the decision, should it just be on BBC or should it have a première in the cinema. We reckoned the audience was going to be much bigger on TV.

MW We've had seven or eight things over the years that have been financed by TV in England, but shown as films abroad. It always strikes me as odd that BBC or Channel 4 will happily put £1.6 million into a TV drama but when you ask how much they'll put in your film it's like, 'Well, 500 grand, maybe.'

BW It doesn't bother me so much. I think the way that we make the films you don't have to have so much money. When I did BBC comedy, you'd shoot like half an hour a week. But when we did *Down Terrace*, which we shot in eight days, we spent as much time with the actors, as we would have done if we were shooting for 15 days.

MW You feel those restrictions are advantages, in a way?

BW Yeah, I love it. I love doing stuff low budget

MW Have you carried on doing commercials during this whole time of filmmaking?

BW Yeah, whenever I can, I'll drop into it.

MW Is that necessary, to support your filmmaking?

BW It is, but it's also just fun. I just like making ads.

MW Have you already shot *Rebecca*?

BW Yeah, that's done.

MW How was that?

BW It was good. It was different. The next thing I'm doing is to *Tomb Raider*. They're all different. That's the thing they never tell you, isn't it? There's genres of films and there's genres of productions. So, in indie filmmaking you have complete control, but television you tend not to have as much control. In an indie film you're the top of the pyramid, but in a studio film you sit back down again.

MW How did *Rebecca* come about? Was it your idea?

BW No, it was something they suggested. I'd been working with Working Title developing other stuff, and it was a script that they had and they

Rebecca (2020). (© Netflix/Working Title Films)

said, would I be interested in doing it? And I looked at it and thought, 'You know what, it's so different from everything else I've done, that "yes" I want to do it.' I try to do things that are quite different, but inevitably they all end up the same.

MW *Rebecca* must have been a much bigger budget?

BW I don't really notice, you know. I found, in a way, that a film like *Rebecca* is harder than a film like *A Field in England*. Just the realities of the day-to-day. The bigger the crew, the more resources you have, the more complicated it becomes. I think the problem is when you make an expensive film for not very much money.

MW Yeah.

BW That's the horror. But making a low-budget film, a film that's written and designed to be shot with limited resources – that's OK. You just have to take your pleasures where you can find them.

MW What was the budget on *High-Rise*?

BW Around £6.5 million, or something like that. I was amused to find that that was classed as low budget. *Free Fire* was about the same. You had a period of making almost two movies a year?

MW I try and do one a year. I think the sort of films I make, they have a six- or seven-week shoot. They're relatively simple, so a year is plenty of time to make that film. All the rest of the time is just where you're hanging around wishing you were working on a film.

BW That's the whole reason, isn't it? It's purely that it just takes so long to get all the money together to make anything. I think, if you can avoid that barrier, then you can make stuff. If you become very fixed in what you want to make, then you won't be making very much.

MW Exactly.

Filmography

2009 *Down Terrace*
2011 *Kill List*
2012 *Sightseers*
2013 *A Field in England*
2015 *High-Rise*
2016 *Free Fire*
2018 *Happy New Year, Colin Burstead* (TV movie)
2018 *Strange Angel* (US TV series: 3 episodes)
2020 *Rebecca*

Peter Strickland

These are excerpts from a conversation that took place on 21 April 2020. Peter was in Hungary.

MW You were about to start a film when the lockdown started?

PS It was ready to go. We had the cast, we had the locations. We were going to shoot on June 29th, but we couldn't get insurance.

MW Did you write it in Hungarian?

PS No, I wrote it in English.

MW The idea is to try and look at the landscape of British cinema . What's possible, what's not. Films that don't get made as well as films that do.

PS I wrote my first feature in 1997 and between that and my first released feature film in 2009 I think there were seven scripts. But you know some of them, I think it's for the best they didn't get made. With other ones – I've kind of pilfered from them. So you can find bits of many of my films from those scripts from the 1990s. Weirdly I have a call straight after you with Film4 about a film – which I've been trying to get made since 2012.

I began working on *Katalin Varga* in 2003, and it came out in 2009. I'd started making Super-8 stuff around 1992. A short I made got into

Peter Strickland, on set, *The Duke of Burgundy* (2014). (photo: Rob Entwistle)

Berlin in 1997. Nothing really came from that. But the scripts I was writing were very different from *Katalin Varga.*

When I wrote them I'd send them off to actors and agents, and no one would respond, then I would forget about them. It's only when I got the email from you that I started to dig out those old scripts and think, 'Oh my god, I stole this or that, from this and this'. I'm sure everyone has countless projects they didn't get made.

But, you know, just to make any film is amazing. So I've learned not to get worked up about it.

MW   I'm interested in the way the ones that don't get made influence the ones that do. Because your films have a very particular kind of feel to them, a very particular world…

PS   After *Katalin Varga* it was fairly quick to get the next one financed. And after the second film – *Berberian* – I was lucky again, but then it got difficult. It was a four-year gap. I got persuaded to do a bigger film, with the idea that if you do a bigger film it can give you the freedom to do the smaller films. But it just didn't work out that way for me. I got caught up in the casting… whatever you want to call it… vortex, I think is the word, where you would fly somewhere to meet an actor, and they wouldn't turn up.

So I was wasting a lot of time that way. Then it collapsed, which I don't really regret.

MW   What was that?

PS   It was a spy film. I was persuaded to write something big, and I never really felt it in my heart, I just didn't feel I had it in me. There's a very particular skill set involved in writing those scripts, and I just didn't have those skills.

MW   Did someone pay for that script, was it commissioned, that script?

PS   The BFI developed it.

Katalin Varga (2009). (© Peter Strickland/Libra Film)

MW   The BFI?

PS   Yeah. And because of the nature of the budget, the producer wanted it to have big stars. It meant getting involved with American agents, which is a world I'm not accustomed to, even though until very recently I had an American agent... only now I've just gone with him to a management company. Obviously for some directors that really works – look at Lanthimos with *The Lobster*, that really worked for him. But for every Lanthimos there are a lot of directors it doesn't work for.

MW   Is there one specific person at the BFI that has been involved in all your films?

PS   Lizzie Francke has been a fairly constant presence, from *Berberian* on. *Katalin Varga* was self-financed up until editing. But Lizzie came

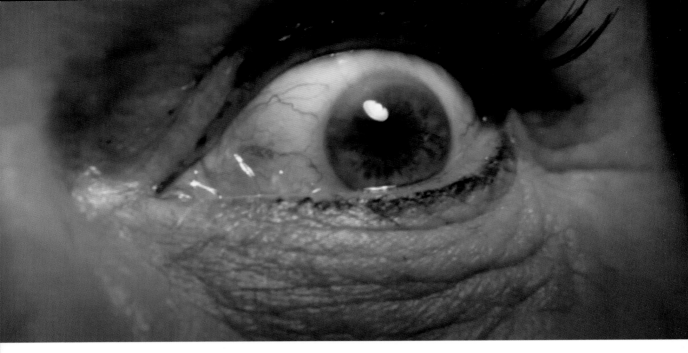

Berberian Sound Studio (2012). (© Illuminations Films/Warp X/Film4/UK Film Council)

on with the UK Film Council for *Berberian Sound Studio*. So she did my last three films and has always been very supportive. We've occasionally had differences of opinion, but she never forced me to do anything and has always been graceful about any decisions I've made. She's also passionate about film and highly knowledgeable. But the BFI want to fund new directors so they kind of nurture you, and then off you go.

MW Go where though? One of the problems of the British film industry is 'Off you go'. But all it often means is that people end up only making one or two films. They're not really going anywhere.

PS It's a tricky one. I can see their point of view. They have a limited amount of money, they have thousands knocking on their door. I think they're damned if they do, damned if they don't. Obviously, I would love their money, I'm not going to pretend I don't want it, but…. You send stuff out, some people say yes, some people say no, and you just have to find ways to get it made. But to get three films out of them is amazing, so I'm nothing but grateful even if we sometimes clashed in post-production meetings. I should add that those clashes always involved other financiers as well, so it was never just the BFI.

In Fabric, which was the last film I made, was something I wrote on spec. It wasn't 'developed'. I just had it in the drawer in case something fell through. We just had the script with Marianne Jean-Baptiste loosely attached and after my spy film fell through, the BFI luckily took on the project.

But it's tricky. My films don't make much money, so each film I make it's getting harder and harder to finance. So I understand the idea of doing something big and successful that gives you freedom. I think it's worked for some directors. I think it seems to have worked for Ben Wheatley.

MW   He has produced some of your films?

PS   He's part of Rook Films, but I fell out with Andy Starke who is Rook's main producer, even though I'm still on good terms with Ben. Just by the nature of living in Hungary, I'm not really close to anyone.

I have one regular person I work with called Fatma Mohamed, she's from Transylvania. She's acted in all my films, but her name can't get a film financed, unfortunately.

With the new film, which we were going to shoot this summer, the budget is a bit over half a million.

In a weird way I kind of like that because I feel I have more control. *In Fabric* was just over two million and it was not enough to get the results on the screen, and it was too much for the financiers to not care about. That was a quite difficult budget for me.

The Duke of Burgundy was like 1.1 million, which was great, actually, that was the easiest film I made.

MW In terms of the actual filming, or putting it together?

PS Everything really. The filming was smooth. No one seemed to argue in post-production, which is quite unusual for my work. Everyone just kind of thought, "Well, okay, it's not a big risk.' There was more at stake with *In Fabric*, so the arguments were more prolonged.

MW How did you manage to finance *Katalin Varga*?

PS Very simple. I inherited a semi-terraced house in Aldershot, from my uncle. The budget was 30,000 Euro. We shot it in Romania in 17 days, with a really stripped down crew. I think there were 11 of us. The assistant director had a house in Transylvania so we all just slept in sleeping bags on the floor. No makeup, no costumes, no production design.

I applied to the Hungarian film fund, and to the Romanian Film Fund with no luck, but as far as I know, the latter helped in the very final stages of the film, though I had no direct involvement in that. But at that point, I didn't apply to any funding body in Britain as I had got jaded with the system, because I applied so much (in vain) in the 1990s. I came close with one script with British Screen in 1999 and Jenny Borgars met me and asked me to come back when I found a producer, but by the time that happened they merged into the UK Film Council with new staff, as far as I can remember. When I found a producer, I was told that no one would trust me to direct it, because I'd only done a few short films. So they got someone else who would direct it, but in the end I couldn't handle someone else directing my script. He did adverts in Hungary, so I went there to look at locations and I fell so in love with the place that I ended up returning for a longer period.

MW What work were you doing?

PS I was writing dialogue for a computer game, but that was in Slovakia. I ended up moving there for a few years.

MW Were you doing that in the UK as well?

PS No, I temped in several jobs, but mostly I worked at Edexcel, the examination board, which was in Tavistock Square back in the early 2000s, and also at the V&A Museum for two years.

It was quite slow prep for *Katalin Varga* and the post was a nightmare. The post dragged on for two and a half years, and then I showed the film at the [Thessaloniki] Film Festival in a section for unfinished films, and one company called [Libra] Film saw it and they put in €74,000 to do the sound mix and scan the Super-16mm negs and blow-up to 35mm. I had been turned down by festivals with the unmixed version of the film, but with the new sound mix and a sales agent we got offered Berlin.

MW How important was Berlin in getting the money for the next film?

PS Hugely, hugely. I don't think I'd be here if it was not for Berlin. We just got incredibly lucky. That was like a honeymoon period, really…

MW I was talking to Ken Loach this morning and he's done 20 films with the same producer, and the same writer. Do you have any similar on going relationships?

PS I wish, I wish. I would love that, but it just doesn't happen. It's the nature of things. I think… I'm kind of embarrassed to say it, I've fallen out with most producers I've worked with. You get to a point, you think, 'Oh my God, it must be me'. But it is like a marriage – actually a marriage is easier. But it would be great to have the same producer.

When I first signed with The Agency and CAA, the normal process is to send you scripts. And I just wasn't really interested. Sometimes it was tempting. I remember a script coming from the Weinstein Company (*The Current War*), and obviously you think, that could sort me out financially. But making a film for me is such a long process that if I'm not into it, I think I'm just going to flounder. I can write for hire, that's fine, I do that on the side, I write for other directors, but directing has to be from the heart for me, purely in order to have the energy to sustain oneself through all the obstacles.

MW You said you'd been trying to make one film with the same producer since 2012. What's that? And why hasn't it got made?

PS It's called *Night Voltage*. It's set in New York in 1980, the very last days of a lot of the gay night clubs in Manhattan, and just before AIDS came. So the last great days of everyone having the time of their lives. It's a lot of money. It's a good five million budget just to recreate those night clubs, all the extras, the music.

So, The Bureau, Tristan Goligher's company, are doing it. Film4 came on very early, they're still on board, but they can't put in 5 million, of course. Then anyone else who is going to commit will want a bankable actor. And it's a quite risky role. It's quite pornographic in places, so I understand it's asking a lot of an actor. So we usually get rejections.

I remember Avy Kaufman (the casting director) sending all these names and a lot were unknown, and they were much better actually, than the famous ones. But we've been forced to go to famous people. It's purely financial. We had this before with other films. We just can't attract the finance with unknowns, no matter how brilliant they are.

MW You've done four features over 12 years with quite small budgets. Is that enough to make a living? Could you live in London?

PS With difficulty. I just calculated my average earnings over the last eleven years since I officially became a filmmaker and it works out as £39,605 per year (after agents' cuts, but before tax), which is good and better than the UK national average, but maybe not enough to escape flat-sharing in London. That money includes fees for features, radio plays, music videos, royalties and writing for hire, and without the latter moonlighting job, I doubt I'd be able to live in London. Within that yearly sum, royalties are only a fraction. My royalties over the last eleven years work out at £652.71 per year (after agents' cuts, but before tax). I can live relatively comfortably in Eastern Europe on that money, but for the next generation of filmmakers who might've planned on moving out of the UK to sustain themselves... sadly, post-Brexit, that looks daunting. It is a huge problem for social mobility.

Even in Hungary I have to supplement my income with writing for other people, which I don't mind doing, so it's not a problem. But I can't make any substantial money from the kind of films I make. When you make a feature film you get a big fee, but that's got to last you between two and four years. And after tax, after the agents take their cut... you can't live that comfortably off it in the UK. The contrarians would argue that filmmakers need to be more productive, but no matter how prolific we are with our scripts, we're at the mercy of funding, casting, luck and so on.

MW Where did you shoot *Berberian Sound Studio*?

PS 3 Mills in London. I found it very daunting because I'd never worked in a studio before. So going from *Katalin Varga*, where we had a camera and a tripod and three lights, to a studio was so, so, daunting for me.

But then you realize you've got a crew. I think as long as you're honest and say, 'Look, I'm not going to understand everything', usually they're there to help you out. There's always one individual trying to trip you up, but in general as long as you're honest about your failings it works out okay.

We won a Silver Bear in Berlin for the sound for *Katalin Varga*. And I think there's this unspoken thing that if you win a Silver Bear they're interested in your new work. So they were very interested in *Berberian*. But when they saw it we got this very polite email saying it doesn't fit the dramaturgy of the festival blah, blah, blah, blah, which I genuinely don't hold against them, given how many filmmakers are hassling them for a slot. So we had egg on our faces. And then Cannes turned it down, and at that point word had got around, so there was almost no point aiming for Venice. It was such a stress. The only festival that would take the film was Edinburgh, when it was at its lowest ebb. And Chris Fujiwara sent us this lovely email supporting the film. I remember having this meeting at Film4 where everyone was in crisis mode and a few of us (including the much-missed Sue Bruce-Smith) were saying, 'Look we've got to take it. No one else is going to offer us a slot'

And we took it. And it was really interesting because it was quite easy to get noticed that year in Edinburgh after their previous lull. And IFC heard about it from Edinburgh, and bought the film based on that. And that was a real eye-opener for me. It took a lot of stress off me in the future because festival rejection is just part of the process. I don't take it personally, that's the way it is. I don't get stressed about it anymore, there'll be another festival if we don't get the festival we want, and we'll find a way to get things shown.

Filmography

2009 *Katalin Varga*
2012 *Berberian Sound Studio*
2014 *The Duke of Burgundy*
2018 *In Fabric*

Mike Leigh

I have met Mike in the past, at film festivals, but the last time was probably at least ten years ago. These are excerpts from a conversation that took place on 20 April 2020.

MW Looking at your career, it looks like you've been able to make pretty much whatever you want, when you want. Is that right?

ML The short answer is, 'Like fuck!' I've made ten films for television, and I've made ten feature films, all of which were made by my saying: 'Can't tell you what it's about, can't tell you anything about casting, just give us the money and we'll make the film.'

And a large numbers of occasions, people told us to bog off! But some people went along with it and we did make all those films – which included *Secrets & Lies* that got the Palme d'Or.

I have made three films where I was very clear about what the subject matter was going to be – and they were the three period films: *Topsy-Turvy*, *Mr. Turner* and *Peterloo*. Although there was never a script, it was still just, 'This is the premise'. *Peterloo* had the biggest budget of all, which was something in the order of £14 million, which

Mike Leigh, on set, *Happy-Go-Lucky* (2008). (photo: Simon Mein/© Thin Man Films Ltd)

came almost entirely from Amazon Studios and they were amazingly supportive and never interfered.

Having done those bigger-scale period films, what I wanted to do was to make a bigger-scale contemporary film, where I explore lots of characters, but without saying what the story is going to be in advance. And that's where we have hit brick walls everywhere really.

It's just been impossible really. I've had people say to me something that I haven't heard for decades which is, 'Well, how can we back it if we don't know what it's about?' And, 'How can we back it if we don't know who's in it?'

MW   That's because you wanted a bigger budget?

ML   Yes. Totally. I wanted to have a budget the same size as *Peterloo* but to make a contemporary film.

Gail [Egan] got in touch with Netflix and said, 'Mike Leigh wants to make a film for £10 million, with no script etc. etc.', and their response was, 'Oh, that's interesting, all good let's have a think about that, yes, very nice. We like Mike Leigh films, blah, blah, blah.' And that dragged on for a while and finally she came back very crestfallen and said, 'They've said no, they can't really make a film where there is no script, and they don't know what it's about.'

We've also been turned down by the BFI.

MW   Is that the first time?

ML   Yeah. They went back to the 'How can we give money to a film where we don't know what it's about.' Which – without being arrogant – given it is me they're talking about, is quite cheeky really.

We had this rejection at the beginning of December and I wrote to Ben Roberts, and said, 'Can you send me a detailed explanation of this?' He said, 'Definitely', and on several occasions I wrote to say, 'I'm still waiting to hear from you'. And he said, 'I'll email you after the weekend, or beginning of next week.' And we are now heading into May and I still haven't had that email, so plainly he can't bring himself to construct an answer.

MW   It seems to me that in general the people who have the money to support independent film in Britain are all quite prescriptive. They want to commission a film, rather than just give you the money to make a film.

ML   What we're actually talking about, in one form, or another, is Hollywood interference, it's a Hollywood mentality – i.e. prescriptive criteria. Anyway, there you go.

MW   We've done several films which were improvised and they were sold on the back of a one-page outline – just 'do you want to do it or not?'

I wonder whether you feel that one of the reasons why you have been able to make your films, and make them so successfully, is because you don't have that development process where you have a bunch of executives telling you what to do.

ML   Absolutely. What you're talking about is the number of films of all shapes and sizes that suffer totally from the fact that before anybody goes out and shoots anything everybody – all kinds of wankers and tossers and camp followers and other monsters – have all made the film and argued it out of existence, and nobody's shot a bloody frame. So it is a great bonus for you where you've said, 'This is a page and I can't tell anymore', and I've said, 'I can't tell you anything'.

So all the films I've made have had that advantage. That's an advantage provided you've got the backing. Films suffer from the procrastination about whether to back a film or not.

MW   Has that happened to you? I've assumed, looking from the outside, that it hasn't happened to you that much. That you've been working at the rhythm that you want to work at?

ML   On the whole, yeah. The bottom line is I have been exceptionally lucky. In the first place, there was *Bleak Moments*, which happened because Albert Finney made a load of dosh from Tony Richardson's *Tom Jones* and he decided to put it into films by young filmmakers. So Stephen Frears made *Gumshoe*, and Tony Scott made a film called *Loving Memory*, and we made *Bleak Moments*.

Then, I discovered Tony Garnett, and more importantly he discovered me, and he got me into the Beeb. If that hadn't happened, I'm not sure whether you and I would be having this conversation.

MW   I hadn't realised Tony Garnett was involved in getting you into the BBC.

ML   Yeah, first thing I did at the BBC was called *Hard Labour*, which I did with him.

Secrets & Lies (1996). (© CiBy 2000/Thin Man Films Ltd)

I then did a whole bunch of things at the Beeb. There was only the head of drama and the producer, there were no other tossers and wankers involved. A producer could do what they wanted basically. They each had three or four slots.

I remember David Rose, for whom I did the second, said, 'How do I know that you won't come up with one that's identical to something that somebody else is doing.' And I said, 'I don't think that's very likely'. So then he said, 'Okay, look. I do all these films about northern working-class life, but I'm from Dorset. So if you promise to make a film in Dorset, I'll let you do it.'

So I made a film in Dorset, which was called *Nuts in May*.

Parallel with all this I applied to the BFI production board to do a feature film three times. On each occasion – because there was no script – I had to go and be interrogated by the production board. And on each occasion it was turned down.

But then Jeremy Isaacs who was the chairman of the production board – said, 'When we start Channel 4, you'll be able to do whatever you like.'

MW *Meantime* was the first one for Channel 4?

ML Yes. Graham Benson was the producer and we said to Dave Rose, 'Can't we make this as a feature on 35mm?' And he said, 'Look, we are going to do that, but not for another six months.' So in fact, it was shot on 16mm, it was a television film. It did go to Berlin, and one or two other festivals, but not on the scale that we would be used to for a feature.

MW Which was the first film you worked on with Simon Channing Williams?

ML *High Hopes.*

MW And you set up a company…

ML Thin Man Films.

MW Was that in order to try and keep control…

ML Absolutely. And we still have that company. It's eleven years since he died, but Georgina Lowe had worked with us in production and she now is my partner and we have the company and she produces all the films.

MW Is that connected with Potboiler?

ML Potboiler was Simon's other company with Gail Egan. Gail is involved with us at the fundraising stage, but she's not involved once we're making the films.

MW How important is it, do you think, that you've had your own company?

Peterloo (2018). (© Film4/BFI/Amazon Content Services LLC)

ML   Totally important. Very important indeed. I first knew Simon at the
       BBC, and we said, 'Let's start a film company', and he said, 'Great,
       we'll be able to make lots of films', and I said, 'No, actually I only
       want to be involved in a company that's just for my films.' Which is
       why he then set up a parallel company, the descendent of which, is
       Potboiler. I've never really wanted to be involved in production of
       any films except my own basically.

MW   So Thin Man is separate to, but connected with Potboiler.

ML   Yeah. We're in the same two offices, next door to each other in
       Greek Street.

MW Having established this system of making films, would you say from then on it was pretty plain sailing?

ML No… I suppose, if I'm honest, there are two separate, different answers to that. In the sense that we made the films… in that sense, you have to say plain sailing. But there's always been issues of one kind, or another. As you know, as we all know, in the end they either back the film and you have the freedom to do what you want to do, or they don't and you don't – and that's the bottom line. So in a sense plain sailing. But my goodness, it depends on your definition of plain sailing.

MW Is it usually the same group of financiers?

ML No, no. The landscape changes all the time. The personnel changes. We did *Secrets & Lies* with Ciby 2000, remember them?

And we took it to Paris to show them and they said, 'Look, we think the film is fine, but you have to cut two scenes that just don't work and spoil the film.' And we said, 'No, we're not going to cut them', and there was a stand-off that went on for a long time. In the end we had a test screening, which, by the way, I'd never experienced before. This test screening was actually in Slough, in a multiplex, and after that Ciby said, 'This can't go to Cannes. We will forbid this from going to Cannes.' But in the end they conceded and allowed it to go and we got the Palme d'Or.

On *Peterloo* it was Amazon and they were delighted with it and said "it's marvellous, wonderful, blah, blah, blah… we'll take it to Cannes.' Then Cannes rejected it.

Then we went to them for the next one but they said, 'Things have changed round here."

So, what I'm saying is no backers stay in the same place twice. Really the only consistent backers have been Film4.

MW How important do you think film festivals are in terms of getting the finance for the next one? Do you think that's a big factor in keeping finances coming back?

ML There is no question that getting the Palme d'Or for *Secrets & Lies* was a massive help in raising the larger budget to make the next film, or the next film but one. No question that that was as important. And you know, a few Oscar nominations here and there helps. But I don't know whether you can really draw up a logical cause and effect of these things, I really don't. It's a jungle, and it's a scorched-earth type of world. You never know.

MW Do you think it's an issue that you are making British films, incredibly successfully, but you can't finance them just in Britain. You still need finance from America?

ML Yes. Absolutely. But on the other hand, film is an international medium, and we do want to flog our films. We certainly don't want to make films just to be seen in the UK.

Filmography

1971	*Bleak Moments*	1996	*Secrets & Lies*
1976	*Nuts in May* (TV)	1997	*Career Girls*
1977	*Abigail's Party* (TV)	1999	*Topsy-Turvy*
1983	*Meantime* (TV)	2002	*All or Nothing*
1984	*Four Days in July* (TV)	2004	*Vera Drake*
1988	*High Hopes*	2008	*Happy-Go-Lucky*
1990	*Life Is Sweet*	2010	*Another Year*
1992	*A Sense of History* (TV)	2014	*Mr. Turner*
1993	*Naked*	2018	*Peterloo*

Ken Loach

I have met only Ken once properly, when we were at the same table at an awards dinner. But, when I was a student, I went to hear him give a talk and had the excitement of having to tell him where the toilets were. And, when I was an assistant film editor, I was working in the same building as his cutting room, and one night had to assure him that I would lock up when I left. These are excerpts from a conversation that took place on 21 April 2020.

MW Thanks so much for doing this, Ken. I spoke to Mike Leigh yesterday, and he asked me to send you his love.

KL Ah, that's very kind of him. Is he well, too?

MW Yeah, he's very well. He was planning to make a film this summer, but obviously that's been put on ice. Did you have any plans for a film?

KL Well, I don't know if I'll get round the course again to be honest, but, we'll see. I'd like to have one more shot. I work with Paul Laverty, you know, the writer. We've been a Morecambe and Wise act for a long time now. And he's a good deal younger than me, so he's full of ideas.

MW He is one of several people with whom you have had a long-term relationship. Are those relationships central to how you've managed to be so productive?

Ken Loach, on set, *The Wind that Shakes the Barley* (2006). (Courtesy 16 FILMS/Ronald Grant Archive/Mary Evans)

KL   Yes. There are only a few of us who've managed to be really independent. I think there's some well-known directors who have had long careers, but they basically work within the system, where they get asked to do a piece, and then they do it. Whereas, I think you and I, and Mike, have pursued our own ideas, or the ideas of people close to us, and found a way of getting them through.

I think there's two ways of approaching this. One – the objective circumstances that prevent a really independent British cinema developing. And then the other way is – how have you, and I, and Mike managed to work within those circumstances?

I have been working with Paul for over a quarter of a century now, and the producer Rebecca O'Brien, I've worked with her for 30 years. And before Rebecca there was Tony Garnett. They've been long relationships and we've worked out a way of negotiating the obstacles. For me, as an individual, the relationship with the writer has always been the centre of that. It constantly regenerates ideas and energy and provides a conversation about what film needs to be made next. What's the idea that we want to get done before we pack it in?

MW   So that process is an on-going conversation between you, and Paul, and Rebecca, or is it more structured than that?

KL   It's the endless, daily conversations. We used to phone each other up, then since the event of the digital world, it's endless texts and emails and a phone call every couple of days, because Paul lives in Edinburgh, and I'm in London or the West Country. And we talk about everything. We talk about politics, we talk about football, we talk about families, talk about everything and anything. And out of that come particular interests, things that make you angry, things that make you laugh. And out of that will come a story, or a situation, or an idea.

Sometimes it is partially a reaction to what you've done in the last one – just striking off in a slightly different direction.

MW Is the process with Paul and Rebecca the same process that you had with, say, Tony Garnett and Barry Hines or Jim Allen?

KL I think with Paul it's even more collaborative. With Jim, he was ten years older than me, and he had some very fixed preoccupations. I met Jim and Barry through Tony. Tony was a very strong presence in the discussions, particularly at the beginning. Later on I worked with Barry and Jim without Tony.

Jim wouldn't leave Manchester. Even when we shot a film in Spain, he said, 'Oh, you tell me what it's like Ken, I'll stay here.' And all his characters spoke with a Manchester accent. He wrote a film for someone else, it was set in Africa. I said, 'Jim, don't do this, it'll only be a disaster.' But he did. He showed me the script and I said, 'Jim, they're all Mancunian, they all speak like Mancs!' And he said, 'Ah, they can put it right.'

So I would go and sit with Jim, and we'd talk through the central core of the film. We'd talk through whether the characters would reflect the central conflict. And then we worked on the narrative. Jim's sense of structure was a bit wobbly, but his dialogue was absolutely from the roots of his being. So I'd work on structure a lot more.

Barry was essentially a novelist. So he'd worked out the motivations and the narrative pretty well. So with him the work was slightly different. How to transfer the structure of a novel into the structure of a film.

Both entertaining and instructive and enjoyable relationships. Both brilliant guys. But both really different in how, as a director, you have to approach them to draw out the very best they'd got.

With Paul it was much more collaborative from the word go. We talk about the idea. Does it get to the heart of what we want to say?

Then Paul writes the characters, and we talk about that. Then Paul writes a basic outline of a story, and we talk about that. Then Paul writes the first draft. I'm always worried when it says 'A film by' and then my name – because, actually, that's not true.

MW Do you improvise on set? Or are the films more scripted than they seem.

KL I think every director has to work out their own process. 'What do I want to see on the screen, and how do I get that?' I try to get a balance between structure and making dialogue which is rich and precise, but which seems spontaneous.

For the auditions, I just do improvisations all the time. Then I give them the script a few days in advance. Then we just shoot it as they try it out and work their way through it. They can start the scene before you get to the scripted bit and then continue on afterwards. So the shooting expands from Paul's writing. But then, when you're cutting it, you cut it right back and nine times out of ten, it is Paul's language.

It used to drive Jim Allen mad that at the end, when the film was done, the actors would do interviews, and they'd say, 'Yeah, we made this all up', and Jim would have steam coming out of his ears, and say, 'They're my fucking words you're talking about'. Paul's much more sophisticated than Jim in that way, he understands the process and enjoys it.

MW Does Rebecca show the script to the financiers – or does she get the money on the back of the idea?

KL We've got two or three people we've relied on over the years, and now there's one main person, at Why Not? [French production company] – and we show him the script, but on the condition he doesn't send it around to other people. It helps that the films are cheap.

MW Roughly what budget range are you making your films in?

The Wind that Shakes the Barley (2006). (© Oil Flick Films No.2 LLP/UK Film Council/ Sixteen Films/Element Films/EMC GmbH/BIM Distribuzione/Tornasol Films)

KL   Around £3 million.

MW   And then Film4 or BBC Film come in for the UK end?

KL   Sometimes they come in. Sometimes not. It's mainly European money

MW   You set up your own film company – Sixteen Films – to have that freedom and control. But when budgets are so tight, don't you find it's hard to run the company out of the money you are getting for a film?

KL   Rebecca's very good at that. On the films we're pretty spartan. You've just got to be disciplined really. Always stick to the schedule and design the film in such a way that it will fit, rather than having a grand idea and then going over the edge. But in a way I enjoy that side, that discipline side... just saying, 'Right, this is what we can achieve and we can still get the essence of what we're after, without five hundred people.'

MW   And you have long and close relationships with people like Jonathan Morris, the editor, and Barry Ackroyd, Chris Menges.

KL   The character of what you do is contained within the talent and the taste of the people you work with. It's the taste of the cameraman, it's the taste of the designer, it's the taste of the sound recordist even, or the editor sharing the same rhythm. It can never be just the work of a director.

MW   When I first started work, I was a researcher on a short documentary about Trevor Griffiths, and I went to see *Fatherland* at the NFT with him. It seems, without wanting to oversimplify, that before that period you made a lot of TV, and since then almost exclusively film. I'm just curious whether you see the TV and the films as essentially being the same. They just happen to be shown in a different place?

KL   TV drama in the studio was quite theatrical. So when we were doing the 'Wednesday Play', those early things, I was desperately trying to do films, and we used to sneak bits of handheld 16mm into it, and cut it really fast, and cut it to music, and all those things to break up this, kind of rather turgid, academic studio drama.

So the TV stuff was cut fast, rough and ready, camera on the shoulder, face the action, get into the centre of it, and so on. Then, I worked with Chris Menges, and we turned away from that and went to an observational kind of photography, where the lens matches the human eye, and the light matches natural light, and you cut when your eye would move, not when the director wants you to look at this... look at this... look at this. And I've stuck with that, really. Whether it is in cinema or TV, to me it's been the same. It's images, it's stories, it's characters and how they interact.

When I worked with Chris for the first time he said, 'What happens in front of the camera is much more important than what happens in the camera. So just let's look at that, and allow it to breathe.'

But *Fatherland* – I really cocked that up. One problem was Trevor wrote in English and then got somebody to translate it and the actor would say, 'I can't say this line. It's like chunks of concrete.' It ended in tears really, because he wasn't happy with the film and I wasn't happy with the film.

MW   I was on the jury at Cannes when *My Name Is Joe* won Best Actor Prize for Peter Mullan. Presumably Cannes has been hugely important in enabling you to make your films?

KL   Yes. Cannes's been massive for us. *Riff-Raff* went to the Directors' Fortnight and it was a comedy and people laughed. So that got us back on the map after the Eighties – a dismal period where I couldn't direct traffic, as they say.

MW   You were still working with Jim Allen for quite a few films in the Nineties. Was Sally Hibbin producing all of them at that point?

KL   Sally produced *Hidden Agenda, Riff-Raff, Raining Stones*, and *Ladybird, Ladybird*. We did *Land and Freedom* after that in Spain, and Sally was the executive producer and Rebecca produced – and then really, Rebecca did the ones after that.

MW   From the outside it looks as though you've been able to make exactly the films you want to make and when you want to make them. Is that how it looks from your point of view?

KL   Yes. I've been incredibly fortunate really. I think it's one of the perks of being inexpensive, so that the people who finance it have a way of being fairly secure in knowing they could recoup what they invested through their television sales. There's a clear path to recoup. So they felt secure enough to put a small amount in. And if there's a few people putting a small amount in, and you're not asking for very much, then you can just keep going. At one stage we were doing one every 18 months.

I, Daniel Blake (2016). (© Sixteen Tyne Limited/Why Not Productions/Wild Bunch/Les Films du Fleuve/BBC/France 2 Cinéma/BFI)

MW You're unusual getting your money from Europe. It seems like most British films supported by BFI or BBC or Film4 look to the US for the rest of the money?

KL Yes. I think they're absolutely wrong. It perpetuates the idea that we are a colonised industry, so you get endless films about the royal family, because that's all the Americans want to see. That's their image of us. And the endless remakes of Jane Austen. They're not interested in what's going on here in real life, they just have this tourist view.

DARK MATTER

With *The Wind that Shakes the Barley* I think we had something around about 400 prints in France, and we had 40 in Britain. Ten times as many in France. And that's still the way with every film, and that's why our finance comes from abroad. And Europe is much more congenial, they have much more respect for the filmmakers, much more respect for the medium, and they don't micromanage. So I think it's been a huge mistaking in looking across to the States.

I think there would be a much stronger independent British cinema, if there were cinemas that would show the films. And the problem at the moment is that the films aren't made because they won't get shown. And obviously TV has closed up now, and the micro-management is much more intense. Cinema for me should be seen in a cinema, with an audience, so that it's a collective experience, not just someone sitting at home in front of a TV screen. So, what we know is that the multiplexes have direct deals with the American big studios. And anything independent that gets in to a multiplex is there out of charity really, or the occasional bit of good fortune.

And the art-houses are now basically Picturehouse, which is Cineworld. So that means that independent films like you make and I make and Mike makes, and Danny Boyle, I guess, sometimes – they're really disappearing. And what I think we should campaign for is political intervention, so that every town, and certainly every city, but every town of a reasonable size, has not only a theatre owned by the municipality, but it has a cinema. It has a bar, it is a good place to go to and it has a requirement to take a percentage of independent British films, a requirement to take European films, world cinema, Latin America, Africa, the whole range.

It would be a civic responsibility, like an art gallery should be a civic responsibility, a library is a civic responsibility, so that the wealth of the culture is available to people. It's not for our benefit as individuals, it's a respect for the medium and the medium is magnificent. We won't get an independent British cinema until the films can be shown in independent cinemas. And not just in the West End but across the country.

Filmography

1967	*Poor Cow*	2001	*The Navigators*
1966	*Cathy Come Home*	2002	*Sweet Sixteen*
1969	*Kes*	2004	*Ae Fond Kiss*
1971	*Family Life*	2006	*The Wind that Shakes the Barley*
1975	*Days of Hope* (TV)		
1981	*Looks and Smiles*	2007	*It's a Free World...*
1986	*Fatherland*	2009	*Looking for Eric*
1991	*Riff-Raff*	2010	*Route Irish*
1993	*Raining Stones*	2012	*The Angels' Share*
1994	*Ladybird, Ladybird*	2013	*The Spirit of '45* (Documentary)
1995	*Land and Freedom*		
1996	*Carla's Song*	2014	*Jimmy's Hall*
1998	*My Name Is Joe*	2016	*I, Daniel Blake*
2000	*Bread and Roses*	2019	*Sorry We Missed You*

AFTERWORDS

PRODUCTION COMPANIES: A PROTECTED SPACE

Talking to other directors in the past few weeks, there seems to be a connection between a stable, on-going relationship with a producer, and a regular ability to make films. Danny Boyle had a close relationship with Andrew Macdonald for his early films, and then Christian Coulson. Nira Park has produced all of Edgar Wright's films. The most stable way of cementing this relationship is to have a production company together. Ken Loach has Sixteen Films with Rebecca O'Brien. Mike Leigh set up Thin Man Films with Simon Channing Williams – which is now run by Gail Egan.

Twenty-five years ago the producer Andrew Eaton and I set up Revolution Films as a place where we could develop the ideas that interested us, and then go and try and get them made. Andrew and I stopped working together ten years ago, and Melissa Parmenter became my regular producer. Revolution Films is still going, but in an increasingly difficult environment.

One simple way of increasing the number of independent films made in Britain would seem to be to strengthen and increase the number of small production companies. This was agreed as policy by the BFI, BBC and Film4 back in 2007:

> BBC Film, Film4 and the UK Film Council, the three principal public
> funders of feature films in the UK, together with Pact, have today
> (14 May 2007) confirmed that an agreement has been reached on giving
> producers an equity stake in the feature films in which they invest.

Over the past few months, BBC Film, Film4, the UK Film Council and Pact have developed and agreed a position, which emphasises and promotes the principle that the benefits of the new UK tax credit should accrue to UK film production companies in order to help achieve the Government's policy objective of creating sustainability in the UK film production sector.

BBC Film, Film4 and the UK Film Council are unanimously resolved to empower the UK independent film production sector to share in the ownership and value of the films it creates whenever an investment is made in a film.

They believe this new approach will help create, for the first time, a real ability for UK production companies to hold a significant interest in their own films and, as a consequence, be able to attract commercial investment into their companies to the benefit of the whole of the UK film industry.

In practical terms, from today onwards, this means that BBC Film, Film4 and the UK Film Council together with Pact have agreed to endorse the principle that in every British film in which they participate, the net value of the UK tax credit created by the 2006 Finance Act, should be treated as the UK producer's equity share in the film, recouping and participating, wherever possible, on a pro-rata, *pari passu*, pound-for-pound basis with other equity funding.

That sounds sensible doesn't it? After all, the vast majority of UK tax credit already goes to global corporations. Surely small independent companies, making films funded in part by lottery money, should benefit as well?

I have searched the internet to find where and when the BFI, Film4 and BBC Film announced that they were abandoning this policy. I can't find the press release. But, for sure, that policy changed a long time ago.

Last year we made a film called *Greed*. It was financed by Film4, Sony and the UK tax credit which was worth roughly £1m. That would have meant that Revolution Films had 20% equity in the film and so, if it had recouped its budget, that share of the money would go to Revolution.

That is not how it works.

You might think, well, OK, perhaps Film4 as a publicly funded organisation spending lottery money, might decide that the 20% tax credit is theirs.

That is not how it works.

Instead Film4 and Sony divided the tax credit between themselves.

So Revolution had no share of the film. And Sony and Film4 had half each.

On a British film, developed in the UK, Sony invested 40% of the budget, but got 50% of the equity.

This has financial consequences. But in the case of *Greed* it also had editorial consequences. Given 60% of the budget came from the UK, you would think editorial control would remain in the UK. But Film4 not only gave Sony half the equity, but they gave them editorial control of the film. This would not have been possible if the fighting words of the BFI, BBC and Film4 press release were still being honoured. At the end of the film there was a montage of captions about the wealth of the billionaire owners of retail fashion firms contrasted to the incredibly low wages paid to the women who made the clothes for those companies. Sony insisted it had to be taken out. Film4 said they wanted to keep the captions, but Sony had final cut so they had to be taken out.

Greed was a film that Revolution Films had developed for two years, spending £100k of our own money along the way. Like all films, it then took a year to make. Then there are the festivals and so on to publicise the film. The production fee for all this work?

£50,000.

On a film being made with the publicly owned Film4 with their policy of being 'resolved to empower the UK independent film production sector' and of creating 'sustainability'… that is not sustainable.

SOME NUMBERS

Most of the money that the British taxpayer spends to support the film industry is given as a tax credit. In 2019, this tax credit was worth around £400 million. The vast majority of this goes to big-budget international productions made by multibillion-dollar global corporations.

Lottery money is channelled to local, British films via three main routes: the BFI, Film4, and BBC Film. Together they invest something in the region of £40 million a year into British films.

On one film, *Avengers: Age of Ultron*, Marvel Studios (a US-based company owned by Disney) was apparently paid more than £30m in tax credit. It is estimated that around 85% of tax credit money is paid to corporations based abroad, almost always in the US.

One big US film receives more support from the UK tax-payer than all the money invested by Film4 and BBC Film in a year.

SOME MORE NUMBERS

A few years ago, I was invited by the London Film Festival to be on the jury giving the prize to the director of the Best First Feature Film. I remember being surprised when I discovered that about a third of all the films in the festival were by first-time directors. Fortunately we only had to watch a shortlist.

This can seem like a great thing – so many people getting their first chance to make a film. The other side of the coin is that many people never make a second film. One study estimated that the average number of films a director in the UK makes over a ten-year period is less than two.

Less than two.

The same study suggests that four out of five first-time directors never make another feature film. Even so, many resources are channelled specifically to helping more new, first-time directors, rather than developing the work of those who have already made a film.

BRITISH CINEMA AND TELEVISION

There has always been a close relationship between TV and cinema in the UK. Two of the three routes to accessing public funding are Film4 and BBC Film. But there is a strange anomaly in the funding mechanisms that distorts this relationship.

At Revolution Films we have made several films funded by TV money in the UK, which have then been released as theatrical films abroad. Our first production – *Go Now* – was made for BBC's Screenplay season – but premièred at the Toronto Film Festival and was sold as a movie internationally. In 2020, *The Trip To Greece* was the fourth *Trip* film to be released internationally as a theatrical film. In between there was *The Road to Guantanamo* made for Channel 4 Drama which won the Silver Bear at the Berlin Film Festival and *Everyday*, also made for Channel 4 Drama, which premièred at Toronto and Telluride. Even before starting Revolution Films, three or four of the TV programmes I directed were then premièred abroad at Film Festivals.

One key reason for this overlap is the TV companies' approach to funding.

For as long as I can remember, the amounts paid by TV companies has remained roughly the same. This is a 'licence fee' system. The rate they say the film (or TV drama) is worth when it shows on television.

So the average rate for a TV drama is around £800k per hour. (If the drama costs more to make then you will have to find the rest of the money internationally.)

The average rate for a film is around £500k.

These are totally arbitrary figures.

What this strategy means for a film like *The Road to Guantanamo* is that Channel 4 offered us £1.6m if it was shown straight away on TV. But only £500k if it was shown first in the cinema. For exactly the same film. That is why we took the TV money. And we then had to battle for the right to première the film at Berlin.

That doesn't make any sense. A small release can draw attention to the film and so make it more valuable – which is exactly the strategy used by streamers like Netflix. If Netflix believes a theatrical release makes their films more visible and therefore more valuable, there is no justification for the publicly funded TV companies, funding British films, to pay such an artificially low license fee for films.

If BBC Film and Film4 paid the same rate for a film as they paid for TV drama – so the average film was getting £1.5m rather than £500k from the UK TV rights – then this would have a huge impact. Many of the filmmakers in this book have made films that cost less than £1.5m, so these films would be immediately green-lit once Film4 or BBC Film were onboard. They would also be in the black, so that any earnings internationally would be profit. This, combined with a return to the policy originally trumpeted by Film4, BBC Film and the BFI, that the tax credit should be seen as the producers' equity, would transform the ability of small, independent production companies to provide a space for directors to make their films.

By artificially suppressing the value of the films when they are shown on UK TV, BBC Film and Film4 force producers to look for investment from elsewhere, often the US, thereby encouraging films that appeal to an American sense of Britishness. They also effectively make sure that most low-budget films are unsuccessful financially, because the main market for low-budget films about Britain is, of course, Britain, and the main place where these films are watched, is on the small screen.

A NOTE ON THE AUTHOR

Michael Winterbottom has been Humanitas Visiting Professor in Film and Television at Oxford University. He is an Honorary Fellow of Balliol College, Oxford and is an Honorary Doctor of Letters at Bristol University.

He has directed three films that have been nominated for the Palme d'Or at Cannes, seven films that have been nominated for the Golden Bear at Berlin and one that was nominated for the Golden Lion at Venice. Eighteen of his films have had their North American Premiere at the Toronto Film Festival or the Sundance Film Festival.

In This World won the Golden Bear at Berlin and a BAFTA for Best Film in a Foreign Language. *The Road to Guantanamo* won a Silver Bear at Berlin for Best Directing and a BIFA for Best Documentary film. *Wonderland* won a BIFA for Best Film. *Jude* won the Michael Powell award for Best British Film at Edinburgh. *Genova* won a Silver Shell for Best Directing at San Sebastian. Six of his films have been nominated for television BAFTAs – three of them won.

ACKNOWLEDGEMENTS

Thank you to all the directors who spared the time during lockdown to talk to me.

Thanks to Ben Pearce for organising the interviews and Holly Mackinlay for typing the transcripts; thanks, also, to Rebecca and Tom for the care they took with this book; and another thanks to everyone who has worked at Revolution over the years.

And finally, a big thank you to Ruth, Anna, Jack and Melissa for putting up with me.

INDEX